Live, Learn and Lead Powerfully:

A Teen Leadership Guide

Chaz Jackson

Manufactured in the United States of America

Cataloging-in-Publication data for this book is available from the Library of Congress

ISBN-13: 978-0-578-43285-4

ISBN-10: 0-578-43285-4

FIRST EDITION – December 2018

Creative Direction: Johnson Tribe Publishing, LLC

Book Cover Design: August Pride, LLC

Editing: White Standard Press

USA $14.95 Canada $17.95

Dedication

To my beautiful and loving wife Amy:

You have sacrificed wholehearted and supported me all the way as I wrote this book. You are the perfect example of a Godly woman. I love you.

To my beautiful daughters Zuri and Mila:

Watching you grow so far has been a constant source of wonder, appreciation, and inspiration. I pray that as you grow into young women, this book will bring you value and knowledge.

To all the young people of the world who value scholarship and education, and the parents, teachers, and mentors who sacrifice for them:

This book is dedicated to you.

You realize and know the importance and benefits of lifelong learning, as well as personal and spiritual growth. This book is written for you as you are willing to open your minds to a treasure chest of information discovering new and powerful ways of living, learning, and leading powerfully, as you are led by God.

Acknowledgments

I would like to express my appreciation to Dr. Adair f. White-Johnson and the Johnson Tribe Publishing team for their many valuable suggestions and contributions to this book. Without your wisdom, this book would not have been possible.

Success is an unwavering marathon of consistency, tackled one day at a time.

#ChazSpeaks

Table of Contents

INTRODUCTION

"Keep your head and your heart going in the right direction, and you will not have to worry about your feet"

Dr. Miles Munroe

You have probably read the title of this book and said to yourself; it sounds pretty cool to learn how to live, learn, and lead powerfully! Or, maybe your parent or a close friend recommended it to you. Regardless of how you got to this point, I am so excited that you decided to invest in yourself and take this journey with me. I wrote this book for you, as a tool that will promote your willingness to become the strongest person that you can be.

Author and Entrepreneur Mark Twain once said, "The two most important days in your life are the day you are born, and the day you find out why." I want to get you on the right path toward finding out and understanding what your true "why" is. It will be one of the best discoveries of your life.

What's your "why"? Why do you want to be successful? I believe that your "why" in life is built around something that you become naturally good at. Your "why" is the purpose, cause or belief that inspires you to want to be successful. For example, there are people born with great athletic ability. Some are gifted with the singing voice of an angel. You have persons with amazing math skills, or other less dazzling and attention-grabbing abilities. Every one of these things is significant today. In other words, you were born with your "why" we just have to uncover it.

1

My goal with this book is to get you on the right path to this discovery. This is not a discovery that will happen overnight and being self-aware of the fact that we all blossom at different times on our journeys is worth mentioning. Some of us figure out what we want to do with our lives in grade school, while some discover it in their adult years. So, if you are a late bloomer, please don't beat yourself up about it. You are not alone.

I want to encourage you to underline the things that are most important to you in this book and reread what you have underlined as often as you need. I recommend that you read this book over and over again. You will discover that with each rereading, you will not only go over things that you already know, but you will also discover something new. It takes a while for things to really sink into your memory, so give yourself time and don't be hard on yourself.

Being on the right path of finding your "why" or purpose in life is rarely one big "Ah-ha!" moment. Purpose can be defined as the reason for which something is done or created or for which something exists. Dr. Miles Munroe taught that purpose is the original intent in the mind of the creator that motivated him or her to create a particular item. In other words, your creator was motivated to design you for a unique purpose to fulfill on earth.

I was almost 25 when the so-called "Ah-ha!" moment happened for me.

I want to share a story with you…

It was Friday morning, and I worked the previous night shift. I woke up around noon that day. My girlfriend at the time, Amy (now my wife) and I were about to go to Las Vegas to celebrate my birthday that weekend as it would be the following Monday. Amy was not at the apartment when I woke up. She had left with a close friend of hers to get her nails done. I got out of bed, went downstairs, and discovered that her friend had driven them and that the car was still parked outside.

Due to poor choices I had made in the past, I had drinking and driving charges and did not have a driver's license at the time. Although I was close to getting my license back in a few months, I still did not have much respect for authority.

I played the scenario in my head; it would only take me about 8 minutes to get to my destination and back home. I would not get caught driving such a short distance. So, I decided to take my girlfriend's car, a Blue Honda Civic and drive to the nearest liquor store.

I purchased some liquor, and I drove back to my apartment. It was a successful mission. I began playing one of my favorite games, Gears of War on Xbox, while drinking a 1/2 pint of Hennessy. I remembered finishing the bottle and thinking to myself that I wanted more. The alcohol began to work on me, and I started thinking about everything negative that has happened in my life. I started feeling sorry for myself and wanted to get even drunker.

So, I got back in my girlfriend's car and drove back to the liquor store.

I purchased another ½ pint of Hennessy and made it back home. Again, I started playing my video game and drinking the new bottle.

To this day, I draw a blank from the time that I got close to finishing the bottle while playing the game and finding myself awakening after briefly passing out behind the wheel of the car. I woke up seconds before I hit another car head-on. After missing the car by just inches, I turned the wheel to the right and crashed into the wooden gate of a church. Fortunately, no one was seriously hurt.

I didn't get to make it to Las Vegas that weekend.

The police showed up and I was arrested.

To this day, I sometimes wonder what made me stay and try to pull my girlfriend's car out of the ditch. I had the opportunity to just run, to avoid another DWI charge, but it was the last thing on my mind for some reason.

The following week, I visited my lawyer and I remember him telling me that because of this offense, I would have to do even more time without a driver's license and face a jail sentence. He told me that I really needed to get some help. I remember the frustrated looks on the faces of my lawyer and Amy.

After we left his office, Amy told me that when I had stepped out briefly from the lawyer's office, he had recommended that she get away from me. He told her I would end up ruining my life, spending it behind bars. He told her,

"Most of the people I worked with that are repeat offenders like he is will "always" do it again".

Amy was considering leaving me since I had let her down so many times. I let my family, co-workers and most importantly myself down.

I knew that a change needed to happen!

Due to repeated *red flag* behavior, I enrolled myself in a 42-day rehabilitation program. It was designed to help me overcome the adversity that I was facing in life due to substance abuse.

It changed my life forever.

There, at the clinic I was able to build an authentic relationship with God, becoming a follower of Christ.

I was able to work through some of the tragic events of my life dating back to the age of five that had become overbearing contributing factors to this red flag behavior.

After finishing the program, at the last group meeting, I remember sharing with the group that it was as though I had a book bag on that was full of bricks when I walked into the program. I was moving slow and was tired of life. It was as though through sharing, and counseling I handed them all one of them.

I went in like a caterpillar and came out as a butterfly.

I felt lighter and wanted to build a fulfilling life. The program had put me back on the path to discovering my real purpose in life. I found my calling helping people through physical therapy and providing empowerment speaking, mentoring and coaching services. My work encourages willing participants to live, learn, and lead as they are powerfully influenced by God.

I find purpose in assisting many to overcome adversity. One of my goals with this book is to give you the opportunity to learn from some of my mistakes that I made and will share with you.

I believe one of the fundamental concepts we need to address to be on the right path towards living, learning, and leading powerfully is being self-aware of maintaining a finished mindset. What is having a finished mindset?

Having a finished mindset is realizing that you are equipped at birth with everything you need to fulfill your purpose and become the leader you are destined to be. You should be excited to know that your abilities to be successful has been tested before you were born into this physical world by the creator. I genuinely believe that you were born to succeed. You have greatness in you because greatness made you! I find the biggest problem that we face in society is having self-awareness of how powerful we indeed are. Having a finished mindset requires the right perception, thoughts, and feelings of yourself and the way you look at the world. Perceptions are the way you see something; your point of view, frame or belief.

An example is a way you view your teacher's impact to teach the class, or your feelings of having your opinions heard in situations or conversations at home, or how you positively influence your family and friends. Your perception of your environment is created by the amount of knowledge that you have. The more things you know and feel, the more things you can see. So I ask, what do you see? Or, in order words, what are you trained to see?

I think it is essential to discuss some abilities that I believe from numerous studies and through life experience that I have found a promising approach to having a fulfilling life led by God. You can make a significant impact on your life and others right now! I want this to be in your thoughts as you read this book.

So, as we dive into these concepts, ideas, guidelines, and teachings, don't be hard on yourself. Remember you are a teenager/young adult and shouldn't have everything figured out yet. This book is meant to set you on the right course.

Theologian Howard Thurman once said, *"Don't ask yourself what the world needs. Ask yourself what makes you come alive and go do that because what the world needs is people who have come alive."*

It gives me great joy to know by the end of this book you will have confidence in making the most of your talents, gifts, and opportunities. You will be able to deal with problems in a positive way, no matter what life brings. You will be on the right path towards achieving success the way you see fit.

I am super excited about sharing these resources with you, and I know you are eager to apply these concepts to your lifestyle right now.

Let's get started!

Chapter 1

Having A Finished Mindset

"To be yourself in a world that is constantly trying to make you something else is the greatest accomplishment."

Ralph Waldo Emerson

Stay locked in for me. This chapter is a little beefy guys and gals, but I genuinely believe it is all necessary. No falling asleep on this section, I am watching you!

As mentioned in the introduction, developing a finished mindset requires the right perception of yourself, and the way you look at the world. Perception is defined as the way you see something; your point of view, frame or belief. Your perception of your environment is created by the amount of knowledge that you have. Sometimes your knowledge and attitude can be way off the mark due to worldly distractions and influences, such as television, social media, and adverse impacts from others.

As a result, limitations happen in our minds. I truly believe self-awareness of limiting distractions and beliefs can change your perception. A healthy perception of yourself helps you see the potential you possess within your physical and non-physical self.

You are worthy of maximizing your existence. Let's also keep in mind that we are all made in the same image and likeness of our creator, possessing the same unique qualities. You were born a finished product, with greatness in you because greatness made you with unique attributes.

A good analogy regarding having a finished mindset is your cell phone. I want you to take a good look at your phone. I want you to notice its shape, design, and the functions that it possesses. Manufacturers of cell phones have one thing in common and that is the fact that they are all "tested" by guys in white suits to make sure it performs properly at the top level. This is all done "before" the creator of the cell phone placed their image (logo) on it.

The creator of the cell phone was confident that when you call your friend after school that the phone will work because they tested it first. They were confident that your phone would send a text to Mom to pick you up after practice with no issues, because they checked the text messaging system before you purchased the phone. The creator of the cell phone is proud to put its logo on the cell phone and say that you will be able to get on your internet quickly because they have already browsed the net on your phone to make sure it works.

Like your phone, you should feel so confident to know that you have a creator that had already tested your qualities and abilities to succeed before you were born. You are designed to be successful, and it is your birthright! The creator placed His image on you with confidence, because your potential to fulfill your purpose is finished and was tested to perform at a high level.

We must uncover and learn how to use those qualities properly. Just like you had to figure out how to use your cell phone for the first time. Makes sense, doesn't it?

Man, that makes me excited to know that I am built to succeed, and it is in the best interest of my creator that I conquer my most precious dreams and goals. Let's not forget regardless of your qualities, all things worth having requires effort and hard work. *I genuinely believe that we all have a spiritual seed within us that has a finished master plan.* Your ability to live, learn, and lead powerfully and achieve your purpose and real potential is in your human function and design.

So, let's walk through some qualities you need to be aware of to have an active finished mindset daily:

Presence of God

An outstanding quality is the need to be in the *presence* of God to develop a proper finished mindset. I truly believe that our body is the vehicle that God moves in. Self-awareness of our Creator's existence and presence within us makes you powerful beyond measure.I have found that when we are in proper alignment with our true self, we produce healthy (positive) emotions and habits. Ways of noticing the authentic environment of our creator within us are seeing signs of love, joy, peace, patience, kindness, goodness, faithfulness, self-control within us and around us.

Pay attention to how you act around your family, friends, and school environment. Are you showing these attributes on a consistent basis?

On the other side, we must notice our unhealthy (negative) emotions and habits. They can consist of always being angry, frustrated, depressed, feelings of low self-worth, and a lack of confidence. These all create limiting thoughts and behaviors. These behaviors can be a sign that you are not acting your true self.

A car battery is an excellent metaphor.

There is a positive and negative charge for the battery to work properly. One needs the other for the battery to function at full potential. In life, you will encounter safe and dangerous situations, people that will build you up and tear you down. As you continue to strive to maintain in God's presence, it is worth mentioning that you are not promised a cake walk through life. I genuinely believe as your car needs a positive and negative charge from the battery to fulfill its real potential, as humans, you need positive and negative circumstances to grow stronger mentally and physically towards your purpose.

By saying this, I encourage you to be self-aware of negative behavior that becomes consistent, controlling, and limiting on your personal growth. *The things that you experience in life is design to teach others, not obstacles to hold you back!*

9

Doesn't that make sense?

No one is perfect, and this is all easier said than done. However, these are principles you are going to be practicing for the rest of your life.

Environment

I want you to understand that the *environment* plays a huge role in your potential and the fulfillment of building a finished mindset. So, let's talk a little more about it.

At this point in your life as a young adult, I realize that you may feel that you do not have control of your physical environment. You may still be living at home with both parents, one parent, or in a foster/group home. I know for a fact there's a guy reading this book living a rough life, in a turbulent environment. With those current circumstances, I know you feel that you must act tough and fight in and out of school to earn a meaningful reputation. You don't pay attention in class, and it is not because you don't care, instead your perception, thoughts, and feelings are that you don't have a voice or any control over of your environment.

I know for a fact there's a young lady doing the same things or even worse. You may be posting images and memes on social media to get male attention. You believe due to the environment you're growing up in, this behavior is expected of you. I know there are some that haven't seen your parents because they are locked up, or you are angry because Mom and/or Dad are doing drugs. I know some of you want to do amazing things in life but have the belief that since Dad or Grandpa was a Gangbanger or made bad choices in life that you are destined for the same.

I know for a fact that every morning you wake up and get dressed, you eat your breakfast, you get on social media to catch the latest scoop on life. You get ready to leave the house, but before you start, you grab your mask and put it on, so you can function in your environment.

Your mask is what you put on every day at school so that you can be relaxed in front of your friends and peers. You laugh and joke like everything is okay, but inside you are broken.

I know you have been disrespected and made fun of because of your looks. Maybe you're not tall enough, maybe you're too short. Maybe you're discriminated against because of your skin color, culture, or lifestyle. I have been there, and throughout this book, you will discover how much more I can relate to you.

You feel as though you do not have a voice!

Red Flag behavior begins to happen due to all of this.

I want you to recognize that you are in control of your physical and non-physical environment. This can be hard to take in, especially if what you have seen so far in your life is oppression and unhealthy behaviour. I encourage you to really take this next thought to heart. **The way the world sees you will always change, but the way you view yourself will last forever.**

I challenge you to work on your life from the inside-out. Allow the spiritual nature of God greatness impact your reality. Remember, you have greatness in you, because greatness made you!

So, I say how dare we bully our peers? How dare we make fun of someone when we are all in the same boat.

Let's realize that regardless of our physical environment, consistently recognizing and paying attention to God's presence will always restructure things! Let's grow our finished mindset from the inside/out.

Becoming

Another finished mindset quality is *becoming*.

When an eagle is flying in the sky, it is not performing a job, it is doing what it loves and what it was designed by the Creator to do: Fly! When a fish is swimming in the water, it is performing what it is intended to and what it truly loves.

You are already born with your gifts; you just need to uncover and develop them properly. I genuinely believe that we are a *gift in a gift*.

Physically you are a gift, but you are also a non-physical gift as well.

I love the example of a *Christmas Gift*.

When someone hands you a gift, it is usually wrapped, and if you didn't open it for some reason, it would still be a gift. But, the problem is you are not getting the full benefit from the gift because you have not discovered the gift beneath the wrapper. The gift inside the wrapping paper is what you spend the most time picking out and value the most.

You must start looking at yourself in this same way.

Our spiritual gift is just as valuable as the physical gift. Along the way to this discovery, you are going to experience and develop a lot of different skills. When I think about a gift; an apple tree comes to mind. What is the first thing that you go after when you approach an apple tree? It is the apple, right? We usually don't care about the bark or the branches or the leaves; we want the fruit. You never see a tree walking down the street trying to sell its apples. It is so popular that people come from all over to experience the gift from the tree. I feel that you, possess that same attractiveness. When you discover what fulfills you in life, you become even more valuable to society. Your gifts are designed to help others realize their gifts and become stronger versions of themselves.

When developing a finished mindset, you are on the path of "becoming" your true self, here are some things to help grow the area:

- Meditating
- Helping Others
- Writing in a journal
- Exercise
- Reading inspiring articles and books
- Drawing
- Praying
- Writing poetry or music
- Thinking deeply

- Listening to music that speaks to you
- Creating in an inspired area (example playing an instrum
- Developing your faith
- Talking to friends that you can be yourself around
- Reflecting on goals

When *Becoming*, you may also experience having overwhelming thoughts to pursue a talent or gift that you possess. I remember before becoming a speaker, I did everything I could to avoid this journey. I would always make up excuses why I shouldn't do public speaking and create videos online to share my story and thoughts. I tried hypnotizing myself into believing I was an introvert and introverts stay to themselves, and do not stand out in a crowd. Speaking and sharing my feelings just made me feel uncomfortable.

The overwhelming thoughts of me pursuing my speaking career would not go away. I tried to block it out, and run from it, but the calling just got stronger as I continued to discover how convincing I was.

Have you ever had a thought you couldn't kick? In another chapter, later in the book, we will get more into visions and take this a step further.

Cultivating

Cultivating is another solid quality of having a finished mindset

It is taking your gifts and talents and working towards developing them to their highest potential.

As humans, we are continually growing mentally and physically and impacting lives around us. The gifts placed in our hearts will encounter a lot of trial and error. Nothing worth having ever comes easy in life. Planned out management and sacrifice are necessary to make dreams become a reality. You must evaluate your circumstances and ask yourself: are the plans for my goals like a forest or garden?

Have you ever played in the woods or a forest?

As a child, I loved climbing and jumping out of trees, and exploring the wilderness. When you think of a forest, the trees and bushes are growing wild and out of control, you'll realize there is not a clear path to walk through. You are running into sticker burrs and don't know where you are going half the time. That is how an uncultivated life can be. When you don't set plans on when you are going to study for school exams or develop a structured path to achieving the goals you have for yourself, you are going to be at high risk of failure.

A garden is a nurtured and cultivated environment. There is a plan in place and objectives towards achievements. You are more aware of recognizing issues when they arise and have a solution to the problem a lot quicker to get back on track.

The garden concept shows good signs of maintaining a finished mindset.

Protector and Natural Teacher

Having a finished mindset develops you as a *Protector*.

The definition of protector is someone that protects what is valuable to them. When I think about the word "protector", the words defender, guardian, and bodyguard come to mind. Just as a bodyguard protects their assignment, you are called to protect your relationships, your gifts, and all the things that you are called to create in your lifetime.

Developing a finished mindset over time, you will eventually become a natural teacher for others. Serving others, when you gain proper knowledge and understanding of your own life is the goal. To be honest, you don't have to be an expert to serve others, start doing it now. You can help by being a good friend, family member, volunteer, etc.

A first-century leader/teacher Jesus Christ once said, *"I did not come to be served, but to serve and give my life as a ransom for many."*

You should strive to serve your real selves to humanity and measure your progress by the positive impact you make in your own lives as well as others.

It is important to address each section individually and meditate on what your heart is telling you. You will be working on having a finished mindset and qualities for the rest of your life.

This book is designed to last a lifetime, and my goal is to get you thinking about the principles early.

Also, don't overwhelm yourself and feel you must know all of these concepts by next week. I challenge you to take things one day at a time and work on being consistent with applying changes to your life. Always remember, this is a marathon, not a sprint!

We live in a world full of distractions, such as television, social media, and other bad influences. What I have discovered so far on my journey, is being yourself in a world that is continually trying to make you someone else is the most significant treasure in life.

As you continue to grow as a leader, let's remember that you must strive to have goals in life and a sense of direction. To live a prosperous life, there must be meaning to present and past experiences.

Strive to live a meaningful life.

Now that you have a good understanding of having a finished mindset, we will dive into discovering your passion in the next chapter!

Review

Let's review what we have talked about in chapter one. As you strive to have a finished mindset, you work towards:

- Being in God's presence
- Functioning in God's Environment
- Becoming our gifts
- Cultivating and developing our gifts
- Protecting and Serving others

Exercise 1: Path to Purpose

The journey to finding your purpose can be fun. It can be exciting and exhilarating as you get in touch and start to understand your *deeper* self.

As you read the questions below, you can write your answers and manifestations in this book, or on a sheet of paper, or you can just keep them in your head.

With these questions, I think you'll have a way better idea of what inspires you, and what indeed makes you happy. You will also have a better idea of who you admire, and where you want to target soon.

1. Imagine 20-30 years from now and you are surrounded by everyone that you care about most. Who are they, and what are you doing?

    _____

    _____

    _____

    _____

2. I want you to think about that person who made a positive difference in your life, what qualities stand out to you that you would like to develop?

    _____

    _____

    _____

    _____

3. If you were in the most significant library in the world, and you had the opportunity to study anything you wanted, what would it be?

    _____

    _____

    _____

    _____

4. List your top ten things you like to do? Literally can be anything-
    playing sports, eating, or chasing your sister/brother around the
    house!

    _____
    _____
    _____
    _____

5. Think about and describe a time when you were deeply inspired.

    _____
    _____
    _____
    _____

6. If you could spend an hour with any person living or not, who
    would that person be and why would you choose them? What
    would you ask them?

    _____
    _____
    _____
    _____

7. I honestly believe everyone has one or more talents. Which of
    these below are you good at doing? Circle or write down all that
    apply to you.

    _____
    _____
    _____
    _____

    a. Good with numbers   e. Making-things
    b. Good with words   happen
    c. Creative thinking   f. Sensing needs
    d. Athletics   g. Mechanical
                                   h. Artistic

i.   Working well with people
j.   Memorizing things
k.   Decision Making
l.   Building things
m.   Accepting others
n.   Predicting what will happen
o.   Speaking

p.   Writing
q.   Dancing
r.   Listening
s.   Organizing
t.   Singing
u.   Humor Sharing
v.   Music
w.   Trivia

8. What barriers or obstacles do you feel are stopping you from maximizing your potential in qualities written down or circled in question #7?

_____

_____

_____

_____

Chapter 2

Discovering Passion

"Every great dream begins with a dreamer. Always remember, you have within you the strength, the patience, and the passion to reach for the stars to change the world."

Harriet Tubman

S o, drop the book and yell three times at the top of your lungs,

"I AM PASSIONATE!"

Don't look around, just do it.

Ok, seriously, don't get arrested for, yelling in that old lady's ear.

But, did you notice the increase blood flow and warmth that came over your body after yelling?

I believe passion is viewed as a stable and barely controllable emotional energy and feeling about something important to you. Passion influences enthusiasm. When you discover passion, there is something within you that provides this continual enthusiasm, focus, and energy you need to be successful.

The word enthusiasm comes from a Greek word ***ENTHEOS***, which means "to be filled with God."

I have discovered on my journey that passion has a more spiritual nature. It works from within you primarily, not from the external world. I believe true passion shows overwhelming enthusiasm. In turn, this shows qualities of love, joy, peace, patience, kindness, goodness, faithfulness, gentleness, and self-control.

Have you encountered someone that is just so excited to share a message? You just feel the incredible energy coming from them, and you honestly can tell they care about the topic they are speaking about. Have you noticed this in yourself? You get an adrenaline rush speaking when you find that person or group willing to listen to your dream or a goal you have set for yourself.

From experience, I know that you will after a couple of years, probably forget the lecture you sat through in your favorite subject in class. You may not recall the senior project paper you completed in English class. Yet, you will always remember how that one teacher/professor that impacted your life while in school. You will never forget that one mentor or coach that made you want more out of life by showing that they cared about your success.

I find it is worth noting that while you are in school, progressing to your adult years, you will discover different passions along the way. If you look at most successful people, they are typically gifted in many areas. You must create opportunities and invest time in yourself and what you find exciting to do. It is critical that you limit building unhealthy habits from external influences, such as internet websites, televisions, unhealthy food, and bad relationships. You can find motivation and pleasure in those areas, but it tends to move us in the opposite direction of discovering a healthy creative passion.

You must be willing to experience different forms of creation.

In other words, being open to learning more about yourself and ideas the world offers. An example would be getting online and searching "list of hobbies." You can create a "list of hobbies" that you are interested in, and ask yourself: which one would I like to try first?

Let's say you picked drawing, photography, basketball, and dancing. Start investing time and allow yourself to see if any of these hobbies could potentially turn into a passion. Research your favorite, or a successful artist, what it takes to perform good sketches, etc. See how it makes you feel over time. As you try different things, you will find what motivate and inspire you to serve yourself and others authentically.

Speaking from experience, most successful people I've had the pleasure of meeting throughout my career love what they do so much that they would do it for free!

Yes, free.

Is there something that you love so much that you will do it for free?

I have come to realize that they are successful because they've found a way to make a living doing what they love to do. If you are genuinely passionate about something and you lack the skills to be successful, make time to educate yourself and stay consistent with growing the passion. I challenge you to do whatever it takes to prepare. For example, volunteer as an intern, or seek a mentor that is an expert in your passion while attending school and working towards dreams and goals.

I challenge you to pay attention to the moments outside of school or work, or when you are alone when you feel the happiest, the most joyous, and the most fully engaged in conversations, books, movies or other life experiences. What are you doing during those times? How do you feel? What were you experiencing? Do you find that times flies by when you are doing the activity, and you are getting more accomplished?

This is a sign of a real passion.

I will never forget two specific people that impacted my life during my grade school years at East Rutherford High. They showed so much passion in what they do. One of them was my football coach and defensive coordinator, Coach Crosby. He was genuinely passionate about football. He enjoyed helping his players achieve their best potential as student-athletes. I was around some fantastic coaches at East Rutherford High school, but there was something about Coach Crosby that stood out the most to me. He truly believed in me and my talent as a football player. Crosby was the type of coach that would always put you first, and if you needed extra help being the best student-athlete you envisioned yourself being, he would do his best to develop you to that point.

Growing up in Forest City NC, I was a big Clemson University Tiger fan. I remembered always talking to him about me playing there one day. We had these conversations on the field and off. Even though I grew up in a tiny town, and top college teams did not recruit in our area very often, he always kept that dream alive for me. He would always tell me to stay focused and passionate about the game, and my dreams could come true. I just had to want it bad enough. I remember lying on my twin-sized bed at my Grandma's house thinking about wearing that orange jersey and jumping down the hill at Memorial Stadium in South Carolina.

My junior year was ending, and the summertime was approaching. Clemson University was having a weekend Summer Camp. I was invited, but my family could not afford to drive me to the campus. Coach took it upon himself to help me make my dream a reality. He encouraged me to get to Clemson's football camp before my senior season. He drove me down, and I had an excellent experience. I remember my size numbers being 6'0 210, playing running back and line-backer, running cone drills, doing seven on seven exercises, and showing my God-given talent. I trained so hard for this moment to convince Clemson University that I was worth investing in. I had an impressive camp and earned respect from the coaching staff. On one of the most exciting days of my life during the camp, I wanted to run a better 40-yard dash time. I ended up with a 4.5 time. That's a very decent time for a running back/line-backer.

At this camp, I met a Western Carolina football coach there. He really enjoyed my showcase. He offered me an opportunity to play for his team based on my performance that day. I remember turning him down, stating that I would be playing for Clemson University after my senior year.

I will never forget what he said after my comment, "If anything happens to you your senior year, and you do not come and play here at Clemson, there will be a spot at Western Carolina for you!" I remember staring at him and saying to myself, I am playing here at Clemson, I am not going to Cullowhee, NC. By the way, where is Cullowhee?

It is incredible how life happens, because fast forward to the third game of my senior season, it was a home game against Ashbrook High. I was playing running back, and I was running a halfback toss to the right side. I received the pitch from the quarterback and started progressing upfield. I got caught up in a moving pile of players, and one of the opposing team players fell on my left leg.

The guy had to weigh 300 pounds easily, and he fell on my left leg while the leg was in an awkward position. I ended up with a fractured fibula bone. I missed the next six games. All my recruitment efforts fell apart, including Clemson as I did not play for a chunk of the season. I guess schools didn't want to invest in a small-town talent, that wasn't promising!

I remember at this point feeling lost. I knew that my grades at school were not good enough to get me an academic scholarship and my parents could not afford to send me to college. I was seeing my dreams go down the drain. Then, I met a physical therapist assistant named Brandon.

Brandon is my second example of someone that showed terrific passion for his craft as a therapist assistant and how he felt about his clients. I was unable to run on flat land because of the fracture, but I performed aquatic therapy which benefited me because the water took the pressure off my joints and bones.

Brandon said, *"Keep your head up."*

He told me that if I did everything that he asked of me, he would get me back on the field in time for the last game and playoffs." He pushed me and gave me life again with his passionate words, actions, and motivation to see me succeed.

It really helped that he actually cared that I got better, and he knew how important the sport of football was to me. I truly believe that he discovered his passion. To me, he seemed to be having a lot of fun helping me and was indeed doing what he loved. I will never forget how he inspired me not to give up and overcome the obstacle in front of me.

I did get back in the game, on time as he predicted. I remember wearing this considerable air cast on my left leg. I was super excited to get back to doing what I loved best. I remember January 2005, coming around and signing day was approaching. It is the day all potential recruits sign with a college team. I remember getting the phone call from Western Carolina football coach. The same coach I met at Clemson football camp. The coach that said, "If anything happens to you your senior year, and you do not come and play here at Clemson, there will be a spot at Western Carolina for you!"

How ironic is that?

I ended up going on a visit to the campus and meeting a fantastic coaching staff and group of players. I received a full scholarship to play for the Western Carolina University Catamounts, where I enjoyed five seasons in the uniform and graduated with the Class of 2010 as a Double Major in Sales of Marketing and Entrepreneurship.

I like to think if it wasn't for God using Coach Crosby, taking me to the football camp, in Clemson, SC, and Brandon in physical therapy, getting me back- on the field before my senior year ended, my opportunity to play college ball would have been slim. The passion of these two men has rubbed off on me and inspired me to push through hard times. They saw greatness in me because they were aware of the importance of the passion within them.

Honestly, they rubbed off on me so much that I am now, supervising the aquatics program as a physical therapist assistant, and working with athletes in various sports as both a Public Speaker and Coach!

We are attracted to these individuals because they have discovered their passion and found their real purpose in life and genuinely care. I truly believe by them expressing intense energy towards their work, they are truly doing what God design them to do.

Directing our actions toward the improvement of someone or something outside ourselves motivates us to succeed.

If you are passionate with an intense desire to succeed, being persistent also comes naturally. Persistence is continuing a goal, despite the difficulty and adversity. Whatever the dream you pursue, you must be exceedingly passionate to tough out the low spots.

Passion is the ultimate driving force behind persistence.

So, let's talk more about the signs that I noticed during my encounters with my high school football coach Crosby, as well as physical therapist assistant Brandon and how it relates to discovering passion is.

It Doesn't Feel Like Work

When you find your passion, you will realize that you are not forcing yourself to do it. One of the secrets to success is building your life brick by brick doing the thing you love. At the beginning stages, you will discover pleasure serving in that area for free, with no questions asked. You just want every opportunity to learn and grow. During the journey of finding your passion, there are going to be good and bad times. Some days will be much harder to get started. Passionate people find ways to keep going and not drag around.

This makes me think of a animated character "Bergen" in the animated movie Trolls (*I watched that movie 100 times with my daughter Zuri*) and how they were depressed, angry and dragging themselves around because they was not truly happy. The bergens looked for outside circumstances to make them happy, but towards the end of the movie, they figured out that true happiness starts from within themselves. So I ask you, what makes you feel alive inside? For you to thrive, you must do things that make you feel alive!

At the end of the day, you should strive to get in your bed grateful for the day. You know that you are on the right path, and you gave the day your best. You can't wait to do it all over again tomorrow. You realize that you cannot imagine going through life without serving in this area of gifting others. With the example of coach Crosby, he was always excited to teach and coach us the game of football. He would come to work very early and be the one of the last to leave the field. He spent extra time working on plays and techniques with players.

Overcoming Adversity

On your journey to discovering passion, you will find that when you are striving for greatness, you will encounter trouble on your way. Adversity is the difficulties or misfortunes that can happen in life.

An example could be that you were working on a 10-page term paper (10 pages) at 10 pm at night. It is due the next day, but something unfortunate happens; you forgot to save the document and power went out on your computer! Now you go back to where you previously saved your paper (3 pages ago) and **overcome** this misfortune by retyping your document (*this is based on a true story, by the way*).

Adversity can arise in all areas of life, including home and school environments. What I have discovered on my journey is that your ability to view the situation in the healthiest way is important. We are all born into adversity. I truly believe as you learn ways to overcome the difficulties of adversity, you become stronger.

With that term paper, even though it sucked to have to retype it, I learned to pay attention to details. It was important that I finished my assignment, so I saw it through.

I can also say, I know when thinking about coach Crosby, he had another life outside of football. Yet, every day he had to sacrifice physically and mentally to be the best in both worlds. Through his circumstances and adversity throughout his life, it made him the person he still is today.

So, to you, my reader: never look at your past with regret, you would not be the amazing person that you are without adversity. Keep overcoming!

Your Passion Stands Out to Others

I love this quote by Golden State Warriors superstar point guard Stephen Curry,

"It doesn't matter where you come from, what you have or don't have, what you lack, or what you have too much of. But all you need to have is faith in God, an undying passion for what you do and what you choose to do in this life, and a relentless drive, and the will to do whatever it takes to be successful in whatever you put your mind to"

I truly believe that on the journey of discovering your passion, it stands out to others.

"You look exciting and energetic!",

"I never saw you so happy!"

"This is without question what you are supposed to be doing to help others!"

These are comments you could hear from some of your closest family members and friends when you are on the right track.

Have you noticed that one teammate that shows up to practice early is always the last one to leave the court or field? He/she always seems to be in the best mood all the time! He/she is still trying to better themselves and others around them because they care about being successful.

Whenever you look at them, there is this place inside of you that gets a taste of enthusiasm and inspiration. That energy you receive from them drives you to try harder when they are around you. When you surround yourself with people that genuinely love and are passionate about what they are doing, it will make you a better person both physically and mentally.

Now as we grasp and wrap up the concepts of those three characteristics, let's talk about the other side of the coin. I have learned from experience that things you see as a passion during our journey can become something you fall out of love with overtime. I know we were talking a lot about my football career, and I can remember throughout high school, football was a big part of my life. I could discuss, watch, and play football every day if the opportunity was there. I noticed as I got older, the sport that I was once passionate about and couldn't get enough of was starting to fade away in my heart. As I look back on my career, I believe that there are two potential reasons I made a 180 degree turn away from a passion that I discovered in life:

1) It was not a real passion.
2) You lose focus on what it took to keep the passion alive!

I lost focus on what it took to keep my passion alive! I went to college and lost the drive and character to play the sport at full potential. I started only doing what it took to just get me by as a football player. I learned in my adult years that to be truly successful in life, you must do more than what is expected of you. I lost the true meaning of this statement. When I was in high school, for example, I would stay after practice and workout without a coach telling me to. I asked to watch a film outside of what coach wanted me to. I sacrificed and invested more time in my passion. When I got to college, I was not consistent with the same efforts. I lost focus on what it took to be successful in the sport of football, ended up partying more, not taking care of my body and I ended up turning into a bad player and teammate!

I don't want you to make the same mistake. I have learned so much from my college football career and it has made my character stronger as ever. I believe being self-aware of my behavior and habits back then has helped to make me into the man I am today. I look back now, at my football career and evaluate the moment that I lost focus of my passion. I think about what it took to keep it alive. There are some things I want to share that I believe will help you not lose focus on discovering or maintaining your passion:

1) Remind yourself daily of why you are pursuing your passion – *better yourself, family, teammates, serve others, etc.*
    2) Surround yourself with dependable people that can hold you accountable.
    3) Stay away from habitual influences that don't positively help your passion – *(drugs, alcohol, negative friends, etc.)*
    4) Write your passion and goals down on paper along with ways to strive towards or maintain them for the long term. Review this often.
    5) Rehearse and visualize what you want to accomplish (goals) towards your passion before bed so it is your last thought at night and first thought in the morning.
    6) Talk about your passion to others on a regular basis.
    7) Always be open to learning more regardless of how much you think you know about your passion. You can never have too much information!

I encourage you to be fearless in pursuit of discovering your passion. As you work towards finding your passion, you will become a magnet for others. They will want to live, learn and lead powerfully with you.

You are destined to make an impact within yourself personally, as well as the lives of others, just like coach Crosby and Brandon impacted mine! Keep in mind one of the keys is to do what you love. You can never go wrong when you imagine big, follow your heart and chase your passion wholeheartedly.

You just have to believe you can catch it!

Now, you have developed some clarity on what passion is, and how to discover it, let's go to the next chapter and discuss what it takes to become resilient in our everyday lives.

Review:

Let's review what we have talked about in chapter two. As you strive towards a specific passion, let's notice things you do that:

- Doesn't feel like work
- Motivates you to overcome adversity
- Stands out to others
- Makes you super excited to share with others and develop your lifestyle around.

Exercise 2: Taking Action

Know your passion, strive for it, dream it, live it to the fullest!

1) What job or profession would you be willing to do whether you got paid or not?

_____

_____

_____

2) What three skills do you possess that you love and enjoy to do?

_____

_____

_____

3) Go online and type in "list of hobbies!

Let's create a "list of hobbies" that you are interested in, and then ask yourself...which one would I like to try first? Give yourself at least 21 days between each hobby, to see if it can potentially turn into a passion!

Hobbies:

_____

_____

_____

_____

_____

_____

Remember this is a marathon, not a sprint!

Chapter 3

Become Resilient

"Don't be ashamed of your scars. They prove to wounded people that healing is real."

Lecrae

My life changed dramatically around the age of 5/6.

I was known as the neighborhood daredevil. I would jump off of couches, park swings, and even out of trees.

On one particular day, my Mom specifically told me not to go outside. I remember begging her to let me go, and she finally gave into me. She told me to stay on the front porch with my little brother Thomas. I was a hard-headed kid, and when I saw her walking towards bathroom to take a shower and I knew my Stepdad was in the back bedroom, I went off the porch anyway.

Some of my neighborhood friends was outside, and they bet me that I would not go up to the top of the street and ride down on a scooter, jump off a hill, and land safely. Of course, as the neighborhood daredevil, I took the bet.

I remember like it was yesterday. It was a two-wheeled white toy scooter, way too big for me, though I was able to grip the handles.

I remember hearing all the kids cheering me on, and I went to the top of the hill, stopped at the stop sign, and turned around. I looked down the road with a determined look on my face. I started down that road without fear in the world, with the wind blowing in my face. I was approaching the hill, going airborne thinking I am about to land this scooter!

Then, gravity got the best of me.

The scooter tilted forward, and there was nothing I could do to stop myself from crash-landing on my face. I ended up face down in gravel and broken glass. I recall standing up, brushing my shirt, off and turning around to look at my friends. Everyone looked and just took off running like roaches in the kitchen when the lights are turned on.

I was not in any significant pain, only my left eye felt irritated. I wondered what was wrong with everyone. We lived in a trailer park, and I remember walking about 50 yards, up the steps to go indoors. When my little brother, who was sitting by the door saw me, he said *"Eww!"*

I walked into the house, and my Mom had just got out of the shower saw me and broke down in tears. She almost passed out.

My stepdad grabbed me and held the front of my injured head. He rushed to sit me down on a stool in the kitchen. It was at this point that I saw blood draining down his arm and began to cry. My left eye was beginning to bother me more.

When the ambulance came to pick me up, they rushed me to the Rutherford Regional Hospital, in Rutherfordton, NC.

I remember staying in the hospital for many days. The doctor's report said that I had glass in my left eye from the fall. I had also split my forehead open, which required over a hundred stitches.

I remember being at the hospital, and the doctor telling my Mom that he was going to have to remove my eye. The way the broken glass was positioned in the corner of my eye, he could see no way of getting it out. They could fly another physician in from the West Coast to perform the procedure, but it would cost a lot of money. My mom did not have the money to pay for proper insurance to cover the procedure. We relied heavily on government assistance and only had Medicaid insurance, so the only other option was to remove my eye.

Talk about having compassion? Well, looking back, I feel there was none shown at all.

My mom was not having that. To this day, I am glad to have a mother who fought to save my eye. She contacted my biological father, who I barely knew at this time. He carried commercial/private insurance.

He was able to come down to the hospital and provide insurance information.

Seemingly, within hours, someone was flown in to do surgery on my eye.

By the grace of God, a man I barely knew at the time was used to bless me unconditionally. I will never forget the day my father showed up and showed love and that he cared for his baby boy. So grateful for him.

My eye was saved!

I remember kindergarten never being the same, after that daredevil act.

Because of my surgeries, kids would look at me funny, call me "Scarface" all the way through grade school. They would laugh and point fingers as I walked down the halls and sat in class.

This happened daily, and I just felt so lost.

I remember going home and crying myself to sleep in my room. I didn't want to go back to school the following days.

I developed low self-esteem, low confidence, and walked with my head down most days.

I remember starting middle school, approaching my teen years, and my life changed.

I grew up in an environment where drugs and alcohol were around. I began experimenting very early in my teens. I was also getting into sports and listening and watching more negative driven music and movies. I was gravitating toward negative behavior. I was able to get away with wearing hats and du-rags starting middle school and found a way to hide the scar that I was so ashamed of.

I found myself becoming attracted to a false identity, so girls would like me. I needed people to view me like a regular kid, and not someone with an abnormal scar on their forehead. I remember waking up every morning, getting dressed and as I was getting ready to leave the house, I would grab my mask.

The mask that I put on every day at school. A mask to cover up who I really was and allowed me to be cool with my buddies and acquaintances. I used to laugh and joke like everything was okay, but inside, I was broken. I had been made fun of and disrespected so much that it became natural for me to feel oppressed and not show true confidence.

As I look back, I wasn't being the authentic Chaz, God created me to be.

This behavior carried on through my high school year, and well into my adulthood. For me, it was not until I accepted Christ into my life, and discover my true identity, that I would find ways to overcome the behavior. I had to allow myself to open up and share with individuals the wounds, negative thoughts, and beliefs I had of myself.

One of the things that I discovered early in life is this fact: *life is not fair*!

Desperate situations can affect anyone, at any time. Some kids can grow up in a low-income environment, while other kids have more than they can ever ask for. Some have just one parent or stay in a foster or group home. There will be times in life where things are going so perfect, and you cannot imagine having a dark moment. Then, the next thing you know, a dangerous situation arises, and you cannot imagine life will ever get better.

You can grumble and complain, but there is not a guarantee in life that difficult times will not come your way. They will appear!

What I have learned so far on my journey is to be aware of what steps I can take to overcome stressful situations when they do happen. Also, I have to know I can control how I feel about the difficult times, control myself during it, and lastly control what I do to overcome it.

How you view your circumstances in life makes all the difference between being successful and not successful in life.

I wish I could go back in time and tell myself not to be ashamed of my scar, and not allow negative influences and behavior to control the way I saw myself. I would tell myself to walk with confidence.

It took me into my adult years to say that I overcame that childhood obstacle, and I am proud to announce that I "love my scar," and confident about not wearing a hat or durag. Throughout my journey, I learned how to build a resilient mindset.

A resilient person is able to withstand and overcome stressful situations quickly. Becoming resilient allows me to develop self-love and recognize that I am worthy of greatness led by God. I confidently can say that greatness created me, so greatness is in me! My goal is to make you aware of some ways to be resilient and overcome obstacles life presents to you as we continue this chapter.

Becoming resilient is dictated by you having a reactive/proactive approach to difficult circumstances. A reactive person is always looking to blame others for negative or stressful situations. Saying things like: *Why me? It's my teacher fault I am not making good grades! It's my parent's fault that I overslept this morning!*

On the other side, being proactive means taking responsibility for yourself and how you can change the difficult or challenging situation you are facing. Proactive people think before they act. They realize the fact that we cannot control the external environment and everything that happens around them, but they can control what they do about it! Sean Covey, the author of *The 7 Habits of Highly Effective Teens* has a good description of proactive people.

"Unlike reactive people who are full of carbonation, proactive people are like water. Shake them up all you want, take off the lid, and nothing. No fizzing, no bubbling, no pressure. They stay calm, relaxed, and in control."

I personally encourage you, reader, to develop a proactive approach. Being proactive will assist you in becoming resilient as you continue to grow into the leader you are destined to be.

I truly believe that!

Let's look at some more examples of a reactive and proactive approach to life decisions.

Reactive approach:

- Responding to adverse situations without any self-control
- Allowing life circumstances to control your behavior negatively
- Making future decisions, based on past failures, or temporary negative emotions.
- Being a follower of others and not a leader

Proactive approach:

- Acting on a situation, before a problem arises
- Realizing that regardless of life circumstances, you are in control of your behavior, and no one else is
- Learning from failures and using the fuel to focus on future decisions actively
- Becoming a leader

So, you are human right? *You are going to be reactive and proactive in situations.*

My goal is to help you realize that YOU have the control and choice to be either one. I want you to be self-aware that during those negative moments, you have a choice to learn problem-solving techniques, and affirmations that will help you overcome beforehand. It is up to you to be prepared for circumstances and understand that every obstacle you face in life is an opportunity to grow stronger physically and mentally.

Let's look at some scenarios that happen in life that will give you more clarity on reactive and proactive responses.

Scenario One

You have been trying to find the right words to say to an attractive person at school that you really like them. You always talk about this person to your best friend, getting dreamy-eyed sitting in class, riding home from school, or even lying in bed at night. You arrive at school one day and see your best friend laughing and hugging this person in the hallway!

You feel hurt and betrayed.

Reactive Response

- Make a huge scene in the hallway and confront your friend for going behind your back.
- Approach the person you liked later, and say bad stuff about your friend, so they don't talk to them anymore.
- Become depressed because you feel sorry that your friend let you down and you won't have the chance to have that perfect relationship.

Proactive Response

- Forgive your best friend, because you were never in a relationship with the person they were hugging. It is possible that your friend was not seeking a relationship with the person you like. They could just be friends. You can't tell the whole story without asking!
- Talk with your friend in person, and let them know how their actions made you feel

Scenario Two

You have a group assignment for History class that will be worth 25% of your final grade. You have two other members in your group, but one of them is not participating and contributing to the project equally.

Reactive Response

- Rat them out. Tell the teacher how the other group member is not pulling their weight.
- Talk about the group member behind their back to the other group members, complaining about them doing their part on the assignment.
- Begin to slack off and not care about the group assignment yourself.

Proactive Response

- Create a plan to complete a group assignment and make clear everyone's specific task to complete assignment effectively.
- Talk with the group member in private and see if they need help with understanding assignment or assistance with getting their section of the project started.
- Communicate with group members and gain a good understanding of each other strengths and weaknesses.

As you can see during these above scenarios, responding proactively is the quickest route to overcoming unwanted situations. When developing a resilient mindset, it pays off to be proactive.

Proactive people:

- Are good at letting things go and are not quick to rage.
- Take responsibility for their own actions.
- Take time to think before they act.
- Recover from bad situations quickly.
- Continually search for ways to keep moving forward during difficult times.
- Stay laser-focused on situations they can do something about and turn 180 degrees away from things they cannot.

You can become resilient, but just like everything else, it must be developed. I discovered the mindset of resilience later in life, but I pray that you read this chapter more than once, and continue to work towards looking at life, in an positive and healthy way.

There is so much power having a positive outlook on life. You become what you think about!

I encourage you to stay away from reactive language such as:

- I can't.
- I have to.
- There is nothing I can do.
- That's just the way I am built.

Continue to work towards a more proactive language:

- I can do it.
- I want to.
- There is something I can do.
- Anything is possible if I put my mind to it and believe.

I genuinely encourage you to share what you learn with others in school, your community, and wherever life takes you. I say this because, I am sure you read this section and know someone at school or in your neighborhood that has a similar story I shared about myself. I'm sure you're familiar with the scenarios and the proactive/reactive characteristics.

You have noticed that person that feels as if they don't fit in, or not living up to their real potential. The classmate or friend that feels they do not have a voice and no one cares about what they have to say.

Let's grab those individuals and let them know how special they are. God wants to move through you. Remember, greatness made you so greatness is within you champion. Let's be the leader and example in their lives and remind them of how much they have to offer to the world. Let them know how rare they are, and they have a fantastic story to share with others! Regardless of what your circumstances are, you can transform into the leader you are called to be led by God.

Remember this, life experiences are designed to teach others, not obstacles to hold us back.

Remember, like diamonds are made under pressure, the complicated times you are experiencing right now are developing you into the strongest and best version of yourself. Become resilient, continue

developing a proactive outlook and be that natural teacher to those around you!

Now that you have gained fantastic clarity on ways to overcome stressful situations and ways to work towards becoming resilient, let's read on to the next chapter.

We will discuss what a vision is, how to discover it, and to learn ways to focus on the gift of perception itself.

Review:

Let's review some key points we have talked about in chapter three. As you strive towards proactive let's:

- Take responsibility for our own actions.
- Take time to think before you act.
- Recover from bad situations quickly.
- Continually search for ways to keep moving forward during difficult times.
- Stay laser-focused on situations they can do something about and turn 180 degrees away from things they cannot.

Exercise 3: Taking Action

1) Listen carefully to your words today. Notice and count how
   many times you use a reactive language like *I can't. I have to. I'm
   not worthy of this!* What is the reactive word do you use most?

   _____

   _____

   _____

   _____

2) Is there something in your heart that you feel is holding you
   back from being happy consistently? I challenge you to talk with
   someone you like and trust and overcome these former
   strongholds!

   _____

   _____

   _____

   _____

3) Is there something on your mind that you have no control over
   that you are always worried about? Decide how to drop it.

   _____

   _____

   _____

   _____

Chapter 4

The Gift of Vision

"Where there is no vision, the people perish: but he that keepeth the law, happy is he."

Proverbs 29:18

Helen Keller, an author and the first deaf-blind person to earn a Bachelor of Arts degree was asked in an interview, *"What would be worse than being born blind?"*

She replied, *"To have sight without vision."*

Vision is a vital key to understand and comprehend. You have eyesite that lowers your chances of running into the wall or assisting you with reading this book. This vision is important, but I want you to think about the vision that allows you to see your future life in your mind before it becomes reality. Your imagination is so important when striving to live, learn and lead powerfully into your future.

We as humans depend on visual stimulation for growth. When you are working towards changing your life, it is important to develop a powerful mental game plan with exact details for how you desire your life to look. I want to make you self-aware of ways to efficiently strive to understand the concept of envisioning goals and values you set for yourself.

I know what you are thinking, I am in grade school, and I am not even close to figuring out my vision. I encourage you to remember that what you see is what you can be. *Thoughts become reality!* It will come to you as you continue to seek it! In other words, vision is the "dream" toward which you are striving to achieve. You hear star basketball players talk about as children seeing themselves playing in front of thousands and shooting the winning shot in championship games. You have heard football players envisioning playing quarterback in the Super Bowl. Those are examples of visions.

I have a daily vision of standing on a stage, speaking in front of thousands of listeners. I don't know where exactly I am, but I have everyone's attention, and they are all engaged at that moment. I am sharing value and empowering my listeners for a better tomorrow.

As I look at my life today, I am manifesting what I need to make this vision a reality. I am a youth speaker and I provide mentoring and coaching services. I encourage willing listeners to live, learn and lead powerfully as God powerfully guides them. I specialize in problem-solving techniques to assist others in overcoming adversity in life. This statement is getting me closer. I love being a physical therapist assistant and it is getting me closer! This book is getting me closer to that vision I shared!!

I think it is worth mentioning that you will have a lot of visions throughout your life. They can be short term or long term.

Examples of short-term visions:

- Seeing yourself pass tomorrow's final exam.
- Having a good lunch date with a parent that you are trying to build a better relationship with.
- Imagining that your day will be filled with positive outcomes.

Examples of long-term visions:

- Obtaining the scholarship to your favorite school.
- At beginning of season, seeing yourself winning the State Championship.
- Visualizing your dream home, job, car, income, etc. when you obtain your goals.

Before we go any further, let's get you a better understanding of how the brain works.

Your mind has both conscious and subconscious functions. It's important to understand them both as it will assist you in getting a better understanding of vision.

Your Brain

The brain is a very complicated organ in your body. We can spend chapters talking about its many qualities. I just want to keep things simple, but highly effective in understanding for you. I want to share with you the concept of the conscious and subconscious part of your brain. I genuinely believe it will give you a better understanding of vision and how to be successful in general.

Let's start with the conscious mind.

Your conscious brain does all the "thinking" for you. The conscious brain also deals with perceptions, thoughts, and feelings that are not habits. Because this part of your mind is not habit based, it is not your real self! You become what you do consistently in life. This part of thinking focuses on one thing at a time, some examples:

- What you are going to eat for breakfast.
- Picking out a shirt to wear to school today.
- How engaged you are in a conversation.
- What movie you are watching.
- What time you go to bed at night.

The conscious brain is not very big on multi-tasking. It is mighty, but also very limited. For example, it's super tough to remember more than a few numbers in your head at one time. Put it to the test:

Look at a random phone list, read three phone numbers off, get rid of the list, and see if you can remember the numbers? If you remember all of them you are a prodigy. Chances are you won't remember most of them! Your conscious brain can lose focus when distractions are present.

On the other side of the coin, you have the subconscious brain. The unconscious mind never loses focus. It is ALWAYS laser-focused! This part of the brain is who you are because it runs off your habits. Your subconscious mind is made up of patterns that you have developed over time. This is an essential part of our human existence, and I will go as far as saying that a lot of us are not even aware of how dangerous the subconscious part of our brain is. I know I wasn't aware of it in my teens, and part of my early adulthood. That's why I want to make you aware of this. Your subconscious brain shapes your life, including your personal visions!

In truth, the subconscious runs virtually everything!

I urge you to be cautious of what you are repeating in your daily life. Repetition of harmful behavior can influence your psyche and create habits that are tough to overcome. I genuinely believe this is why some people end up in difficult circumstances, or not living the life they truly desire. As time goes on, they say to themselves,

"What happened and how did I get here?"

They got there running on autopilot.

For example, have you been on your way home, taking the same route for school for months/years, thinking about something that happened at school (arguing with a close friend), and pulled up to your house. All of a sudden, you realize that you are home, and you're freaked out because you don't remember making that right turn by the convenience store.

Yes, your route home is downloaded into your subconscious the same way you can download your favorite computer game and save it on your computer. Once the game is saved on the computer, it doesn't have to spend the 30 minutes to an hour downloading onto the hard-drive anymore. It will start up right away.

Makes sense?

Again, the *subconscious is automatic and is influenced by repetition.* You must be conscious of your choices daily and what you download on your personal hard-drive! This is important for your inner vision to grow.

So, another example, if your conscious brain is like the leading scroll light, shining on your favorite singer on stage, then your subconscious mind is like the main auditorium or arena light, that is cut on after the concert, so you can see clearly and can leave safely. This is possible only on a subconscious level (which means you are not aware of it.) Both the conscious and unconscious brain have significant effects on your imagination and vision for your life.

Please keep this in mind and review as you continue to read this book. Again, this is very important when discovering the gift of vision!

The Farmer's Vision

Now that you have a better understanding of the conscious and subconscious brain, let's dive deeper into the conversation of understanding vision.

After numerous studies about the concept of vision, I have developed a unique story that's helped me understand the idea. I hope you find some benefit out of it, as you continue your journey.

I want you to keep an open mind with me and build a clear picture in your mind as I explain this scenario.

Imagine that you are a farmer, before fast food restaurants, electronics, and the internet. You own five acres of land where you have cows, pigs, horses, chickens, and sheep that you take care of and protect daily. You have a barn on the property.

You also have a garden where you grow vegetables like tomatoes and cucumbers that you sell in town. You also feed your family with the produce you grow.

After some thought, you have decided to grow some more trees behind your house. You have a different seed that you purchased in town last year. You chose to plant the seed today, and you are super excited about it. As a good farmer should, you nurture, water, fertilize, and make sure the seed is able to get good sunshine.

Once the seed is in the ground, you cannot stop thinking about it. Daily images of seeing the tree break surface and grow into a beautiful creation are on your mind. You see clear pictures of it when you lay in bed at night.

The first year passes by, and no growth happens!

As a farmer, you continue to take care of the seed. The second year comes and no increase. The third and fourth years come, and no growth.

You are passed being frustrated at this point. Thoughts of giving up are on your mind, but you have seen the vision of this beautiful tree already. Your faith does not allow you to give up. So, you stay committed to your idea. You continue to nurture and water the seed.

Then, in the fifth year, something magical happens. The tree breaks the surface! You can hardly believe it. The tree begins to grow at a fast rate. In five weeks, the tree grew 90 feet! Your unseen vision became a reality.

Years later, you discovered that the tree takes so long to sprout because it has to develop the necessary roots in the ground. It has to be able to support itself when it breaks surface externally, or in other words in the visual world.

I genuinely believe with all my heart, that the farmer in this scenario gives you a good illustration of how to approach your vision. The seed is a good illustration of the vision itself.

Let's talk about some examples the farmer showed you in the scenario that you can use in your approach towards making your vision a reality:

- The vision is always on your mind day and night.
- You are excited about pursuing the dream or goal.
- You find yourself developing skills that will equip you in bringing the vision to reality.
- You are willing to do whatever it takes if it contributes to the development of your vision.
- Things begin to fall into the right place, even at times when you feel tired, and there's no hope for success.

- You didn't give up, even though it took many years to manifest.
- You showed consistent, proactive behavior (mentioned in chapter 3.)

The farmer was very clear on what he wanted and acted on making the unseen a reality. The farmer nurtured and cherished the seed and showed excitement when pursuing his goal. You must imagine that during this five-year process, that the farmer's family and friends tried to convince him to give up on the seed telling him it is a bad seed.

Doubts went through the farmer's mind after years of seeing no growth, but the farmer did not let bad behavior set in or change the heart when it came to his vision of the tree.

The farmer maintained good thinking habits and kept the faith in God that his picture of a beautiful tree in mind would come to reality.

Now let's take a look at the scenario from the seed perspective.

Again, I believe the seed is a good illustration of the vision itself because:

- It shows that vision requires proper development and protection to grow.
- It involves patience from visionary.
- It requires self-discipline from visionary.
- It will not develop properly unless it has the support (roots) to withstand reality (life choices and circumstances.)
- It needs the visionary to maintain consistency and not dig up the seed and plant elsewhere.

The seed is as strong as the farmer!

When talking about the seed within you, it requires patience and self-discipline to transition from just being imagery or just a dream to reality. Remember from earlier in the chapter, I mentioned when you are working towards changing your life, it is important to develop a powerful mental game plan with exact details for how you desire your life to look.

This is an excellent thing, but what tends to happen a lot of times is within weeks or days, of planting you can become discouraged or lose sight of the vision. Things don't go the way you planned, or it turns out that it is going to be harder than you thought.

Like the example of the farmer, there was no growth for four years! Many of us would have said forget it days, months or a year in. Many would have given up, or dug the seed up and planted elsewhere, but the farmer believed in his vision and continued to do his part as a cultivator and protector and allowed God to do the rest.

I genuinely think that as long as the roots of your seed within are sincere, your reality will manifest and there will be no wind (distractions or doubts) that can knock your tree down.

I want to provide some other helpful ways that we will discuss in more detail throughout this book or some in the actual chapter itself. Some methods you can apply now are:

- Set goals (writing ideas down.)
- Seek mentors and coaches that show the qualities it will take to reach your vision successfully.
- Help others make their vision a reality.
- Create a bright idea or picture.
- Surround yourself with others that will benefit in making your vision a reality.
- Focus on it often.
- Build a relationship with our Creator.
- Meditate.
- Give it positive energy.
- Do affirmations that keep you maintaining a healthy mindset towards your vision.
- Supporting desire, belief, and acceptance that you CAN have the image.

I pray that you can get a good idea and understanding of the information above.

It is a proven fact that without a vision for where you are going in life, you will be setting yourself up to crumble. People with big visions and dreams become unstoppable, and those without a vision walk through life in a state of anger and confusion. I truly believe the information we have talked about will get you on the right path. Anything you can envision clear enough and long enough, like the farmer in the example, you can make happen!

I want to finish up this chapter by introducing an understanding of time and energy. This information will also help you maintain a healthy vision, and prosperous outlook on life.

Time and Energy

As you work on making your unseen vision a reality, whether it is a short-term or long-term vision, you have to realize a significant thing.

Time and energy are the only two things you indeed have control over. When I discovered this truth well into my adulthood, it changed my whole perspective and outlook on life. I believe it would have made a massive difference in my life if discovered in my teens.

As you may know, on a physical level, you only have a specific time frame to exist on the earth. Research shows that the average adult in America lives about 76.5 years. Now I know you are young, and it seems like a long time away looking from the eyes of a teenager or young adult. It is much less than that. Did you know that if you sleep seven hours per night that eliminates about 25 years off your life? It blew me away thinking that I will be spending more than 33% of my life sleeping!

Now, I am not saying to drink a bunch of coffee or a Red Bull daily to try to stay up as late as possible every night. Sleep is very important on a physical and mental level. I want you just to be self-aware of how sensitive and valuable your time on this earth is.

Again, all you have is your time and energy, and as we talked about in an earlier chapter being proactive is one of the golden keys towards saving time and success.

I urge you early in life to be aware of your time and energy. When you read books, such as this one, you are investing your time and energy. When you are working towards graduating high school, you are spending your time and energy. The moments you are wasting time arguing with your friend over the phone or making bad decisions that are not benefiting from your vision and goals, you are investing time and energy. When you spend time with your friends and family that brings you joy, you are investing your time and energy. When you are envisioning your passion, you are investing your time and energy. Whether the situation is negative or positive, self-awareness of time and energy and making the best of it is crucial.

Ask yourself this daily…what I am spending my time and energy on right now, is it a healthy habit or mental junk-food (unhealthy habit?)

Everything in life starts first with thought and imagination before it becomes a reality. I encourage you to think outside the box by moving your mind and emotions into the environment of unlimited possibilities. With God all things are possible. Strive to make that a clear understanding within your heart!

I hope you found this chapter helpful in working towards making your unseen vision a reality. Let's continue to strive to be complete people and inspire others to find that balance in life.

Let's move on to the next chapter and learn how to build your life around values.

Review

Let's review some key points we have talked about in chapter four. When discovering and understanding the gift of vision:

- Vision is the "dream" that you are striving to achieve.
- The Conscious brain can lose focus when distractions are present.
- The subconscious mind does not lose focus. It shapes most of your life decisions.
- By saying this, the most important thing to remember is to pay attention to what habits good or bad shape your subconscious decisions.
- You can have multiple visions in your lifetime, some short-term and long-term.
- A vision requires proper developing and protection to grow.
- Focus on what and where you spend your time and energy

Exercise 4: Take Action

1) Pay attention to your efforts when going after that vision you are envisioning. How can you work on applying the mindset of the farmer?

_____
_____
_____
_____

2) List your top ten things that take up most of your time and energy. Is it promoting the growth of your vision?

1.

2.

3.

4.

5.

6.

7.

8.

9.

10.

Chapter 5

Build Your Life Around Values

"It is impossible for us to break the law, we can only break ourselves against the law."

Cecil B. DeMille

So, here you are.

You are young and have your whole life before you. Imagine yourself driving down the highway of growth, and it is up to you to choose which exit to take!

You will get advice from many, but you are ultimately in charge of YOUR path.

- Do you plan to finish high school? Go to college?
- Should you join an extra-curricular activity?
- Should you date, and if so what kind of person?
- What type of friends do you want to be around?
- Will you drink, smoke, and/or do drugs?
- What will be your attitude towards life?
- Will you skip school with your friends?
- Will you have sex before marriage?
- Will you have a good relationship with your family?
- How will you serve your community?
- Will you choose to like yourself?
- What will you stand for?

I challenge you to honestly answer those questions above and realize that the paths you choose today, will impact your life forever. Honestly, it will be both frightening and exciting. You will make so many decisions, some good and some bad, during your years of teenage-hood!

Good decision-making is influenced by values. So, what are values?

Values are a list of beliefs or standards, that you personally choose to follow, and apply to your lifestyle. It is what you are going to use as your life foundation, which will assist in shaping your attitude and character towards making life decisions. What's important to you?

Let's imagine that you are about to graduate high school, and your parents decide to get you a car as a graduation present.

Your mom and dad ask, "What size car do you want?"

You kind of shrug your shoulders and say, "Huh, a medium size one."

Your parents ask, "What color car do you want?"

You say while scratching your head, "Well, like a greenish color!"

Lastly, your Dad asks, "How many seats would you like?"

You say, "Well seats are important, will need one to drive right!"

The whole time you are confused about what you truly want. Graduation Day comes, and your Parents are standing outside with this car that you honestly don't really like. The car is not big enough to carry all your stuff to college in the Fall. It is a two-door car, so all your friends won't get to ride. You are also not a fan of the light green color.

Even though your parents gave you the opportunity to get what you wanted, you did not think about, plan, nor provide specific details on what you truly desired.

You can go through life in this fashion. You don't plan for things, super confused about life decisions, and just let things happen as it goes.

Having core values in place gives you a foundation and allows you to set a successful plan to follow. A person with values holds themselves accountable to authentic standards, and their personal actions daily. They create behaviors that match the value itself.

For example, you could value being committed to making good grades in school or maintaining honesty when having conversations with family and friends. I truly believe that applying values to something more significant is one of the keys to success!

So, I ask you, what kind of benefits do you hold yourself accountable to?

What are some of your family values?

Some family values, for example, could be:

1. Being honest when having conversations with each other.
2. Eating dinner together at a specific time every night as a family.
3. Not taking things that don't belong to you (stealing).
4. When up to the appropriate age, getting a job and learning to maintain a steady living for yourself and family.

Another example of applying values to your lifestyle is the High School Baseball Team Coach who holds himself and baseball players accountable for becoming persons of "integrity."

Integrity means holding yourself accountable to make sound decisions. The team would be focused on reliably doing the right things. That benefits the team's success and won't dishonor or demean them or their teammates. The coach strives to make players aware of being faithful to the game of baseball and their lives outside of the sport. It is essential to understand that values in life cannot be broken or changed! Only you as an individual can break yourself against the values. In other words, just your perceptions, thoughts, or feelings about the value or how you approach your decision-making towards the value you chose to live by will change.

Now, going back to the value of integrity.

If I am striving to do the right things, in a reliable way that wouldn't jeopardize my position on the baseball team, I would consistently align my decision making around living by integrity, especially when presented the opportunity to break the law by stealing. Even though I don't have any money and really want the candy bar at the store, I am self-aware of how much I value integrity, as well as my team's integrity. Everything could be at stake based on my decision-making.

This example makes me think about a life experience I had at the age of 14/15. It involved stealing.

My parents and grandparents did the best they physically and mentally knew how to raise me and provide for me. During this stage in my life, I would see other kids wearing the latest trends in fashion at school. In my eyes, my clothing didn't measure up. All was a blessing to have, but I wanted more, and I was not able to afford it.

One of my good friends and I were dealing with similar thoughts. Together, we decided that we were going to take the chance of taking what didn't belong to us. So, we started breaking the law by stealing.

One Saturday, we decided to go to the Mall. We didn't drive at the time, so we walked about 45 minutes to an hour to get there. We window-shopped and went into different stores, one of them specializing in selling upscale clothing and jewelry. We were both looking around, and I spotted an amazing watch on a nicely laid out table presentation to the left of the entrance door. It had lots of stones (cubic zirconia) on the face and was paired with a beautiful black band. The stones on the watch were not real, but in my mind at the time, they were expensive diamonds sparkling at me.

There was something inside of me that was saying *don't do it*. Yet, the other side of me couldn't resist, and I started looking around for the store workers.

There was one guy working in the jewelry department. I was focused on his location, started signaling for my friend to let him know what I was about to do. I planned to take the watch and make my way towards the entrance with the store worker facing away from my position.

"Don't do it, Chaz," a small voice in my head was telling me, but I ignored it, and kept telling myself that this is easy.

Everyone at school will think I am so cool with this watch. All the girls will flock to me if I have this watch.

I won't get caught, I thought to myself.

So, I grabbed the watch, heart beating out of my chest, stuck it in my pants pocket, and my friend and I ran towards the exit.

We made it out the door, and then the unexpected happened.

"You kids turn back around and go back in the store."

My heart dropped, and I looked at my friend.

We just got caught! They had been watching us the whole time on camera, and we were not aware of it. Our plans for a great escape have worked in the past, but not today. Next thing I knew, I was handcuffed and riding in the back of a Police Car. They took us to the Downtown Police Department where they placed us in separate holding cells. The cell was a very small area with one little light, so it was somewhat dark. It had about ten-fifteen metal poles at the door, and a short stone bench that was cold to sit on.

It finally kicked in that I was sitting in a jail cell!

The Police told me that I would stay here until my guardian was able to come to get me. I was there for one hour or so, but it felt like the most extended hour of my life. I felt so low and ashamed of what I did. How would I face my Mom and Grandma? What will my Coach and teammates think if they find out? At the time I was saying to myself, I rather just stay in here than face my grandma!

I ended up being placed on probation and doing fifty hours of community service at our local thrift store.

As mentioned earlier in the chapter, *we don't break the law, we break ourselves against the law*. The law of stealing never changes, but my life after that incident changed forever.

I am grateful that my Coach allowed me to continue the football team. I realize as an adult now that I did not have any self-discipline to recognize that my decisions not only affected me, but others as well. Later in life, I found myself locked up in jail on other occasions, for even more extended periods of time.

One day, I decided to make a change led by God. I realized the power of making the right decisions when presented with a negative or tempting one shows self-discipline.

For example, not choosing the path of stealing shows self-discipline.

It is so worth mentioning that being focused requires self-discipline and self-control. During the times of adversity in school and life in general, the values that you hold yourself accountable to will be challenged. Developing self-discipline as you strive towards your passions, visions, or just making healthy daily decisions will be vital.

Let's talk about discipline in three different parts: mental, emotional and physical.

MENTAL DISCIPLINE

Mental Discipline is striving to maintain your focus when distractions are present. It is the ability to stay laser-focused on whatever task you're performing (taking a test at school, conversation with a parent, etc.) so that you do it in the right way. It is being present in the moment, which allows you to function effectively and efficiently.

When I think about being mentally disciplined, the sport of Basketball comes to mind.

I think of NBA superstar Stephen Curry. He is leading the league in free throw shooting percentage, with 92.1% in 2018. That is an incredible number!

Imagine this: He's down by one point in the fourth quarter, one second left on the clock. He is not playing on his home court, so the fans are going crazy behind the scoreboard. They are trying their best to be a distraction to him, so he will miss the two shoots, or at least one. They want the game to be tied so that it goes into overtime.

Because Steph Curry relentlessly practices free-throws on his own time, he has developed the mental discipline to make the big shots when it matters most.

He makes both free-throws due to his laser-focus and trained skill.

Are you laser-focused?

EMOTIONAL DISCIPLINE

Striving to limit run-a-way thoughts and control your negative emotions and feelings is a very tough task. It is an even more difficult task to build the habit of making thoughtful choices that serve your core values.

So, this brings back a funny memory that I want to use as an example of emotional discipline.

Well, it is funny now, but it was not at the time.

I was around 16/17 years old and I wanted to go out with my friends on a Friday night. My grandmother told me I could go hang out, but to get home before 10 o'clock. I nodded my head in agreement as I was leaving.

I remember riding later that night with my friends and my homeboy asked if I wanted to go to the bowling alley. The bowling alley was a favorite hangout for us teenagers at the time. If you know Forest City, NC, there is not a lot of places to hang out. I was having *run-a-way thoughts* and really wanted to hang out with my friends. I was thinking, it is not fair I have to go home, and everyone else's parents are not so strict. I let my emotions take over, and I began to get frustrated and angry when I thought about my Grandma giving me the curfew.

I told my friend, "Yes, let's go to the bowling alley."

I figured my grandmother would be asleep and I will just sneak in the trailer. I came up with a master plan! The way the trailer is set up, when I walked through the front door, my room is to the right, and hers is back far to the left. So, I planned to be as quiet as possible. No turning lights on or making stops to the bathroom. There would be no going to the refrigerator (I was hungry too.) It was after 12 pm, and the plan was in effect. I came through the front door, headed to the right, walking as quietly as possible. I saw the light at the end of the tunnel, I thought I was going to make it to my room and be in the clear, when I heard an unhappy voice say,

"Chaz, get your butt back in here."

My heart dropped. It was my grandmother. She was awake!

I started walking back to the front room. She flipped on the light switch and I saw that she had a broom in her hand. She was furious.

My grandmother never played softball (at least I don't think so), but she was a strong lady and had a heck of a swing.

I let my emotions get the best of me when I was around my friends. I was more emotionally worried about being cool and hanging out with them instead of staying disciplined and obeying my grandmother's rules she set for our home. As I look back on my journey, I realize that it is essential to become aware of your emotions and allow core values to outweigh your feelings.

PHYSICAL DISCIPLINE

The ability to make yourself do something when you should do it, whether you feel like or not, is a sign of you striving to nurture your physical happiness. That is you realizing that your values should ALWAYS outweigh your negative feelings and thoughts.

The concept of physical discipline makes me think back to my Freshman year of football training camp at Western Carolina University in 2005.

I honestly did not train very often that summer after high school graduation and I was out of shape. The first day of college football camp, during the conditioning test was horrible. I thought I was going to die! We consistently ran, lift weights, practiced, watched the film, and had set plans and priorities that we had to follow as a team. The team would wake up at 4:30-5:00 am every morning and do it all over again! I was so sore and could barely get out of bed.

I had never experienced anything like it in my life up to that point. It got to a point during that training camp that I was on the path of quitting.

The thoughts grew stronger when one of my close friends threw in the towel and quit! I was thinking of all kind of things to do to make a living if I went back home.

I said to myself,

"I can just go to the Army,"

"I can do job corps, and study a trade, or go to community college for a while."

With Head Football Coach Briggs' and my grandmother's consistent motivation, I kept my head above water that year.

The coach shared a quote daily that helped me get through that camp.

He said,

"Pain is temporary, giving up is forever."

He would say over and over every day, and so, it stuck with me.

I began to use that as a value and learned to push through. I realized when I overcame this obstacle it would be so worth it. I held on to the big picture of trying to be the best I could be for myself, and the family who was depending on me. I can say proudly that I showed the ability to make myself do something, whether I felt like it or not. I am not perfect, but I learned to allow my mind to motivate my body through adversity.

I strive to carry the same discipline to this day. I realize as an adult, sometimes your greatest pain is not even about you. It is about a higher purpose. If you can find a way to push through the adversity and not make it about you, there will be something special waiting for you on the other side.

I have personally learned to enjoy the occasional storms, just like my favorite bird, the Eagle. The eagle is the only bird in the bird kingdom that stays out when a storm is appearing. They soar across the sky, using no physical strength to keep elevated. They respond without fear or doubt that lightning is going to strike them. I believe that they are so confident because they genuinely think that something higher than themselves (God) is protecting over them. All the other birds known to man will run and hide in the trees, or other safe places.

Not the Eagle.

Seek to love storms like the Eagle and remember that diamonds are made under pressure. God is making a masterpiece of you!

Some other values and a brief example with each that you could hold yourself accountable to in school/work/community include:

- Connection   *e.g. When I am in a new environment, I will try meeting new people*
- Compassion   *e.g. I will listen more during conversations*
- Determination   *e.g. Focus on finishing projects and assignments*
- Education   *e.g. Reading homework chapters before the next class period*
- Empowerment   *e.g. Listening to motivational music or speeches to start the day*
- Equality   *e.g. Focus on being fair to others*
- Family   *e.g. Setting time out to spend with people I love*
- Flexibility   *e.g. Don't overcommit*
- Fun   *e.g. Be open to new experiences*
- Genuine   *e.g. Smile when you pass someone*
- Gratitude   *e.g. Give thanks for all your blessings*
- Hard work   *e.g. Plan and take action*
- Honesty   *e.g. Tell the truth during conversations*
- Inner Peace   *e.g. Focus on a healthy mindset*
- Love   *e.g. Caring for others as yourself*
- Loyalty   *e.g. Focus on keeping your promises to others*
- Optimism   *e.g. Do positive affirmation in the mornings*
- Trust   *e.g. Focus on being consistent*
- Passion   *e.g. Do things that don't feel like work*
- Uniqueness   *e.g. Try not to be like anyone else. Be yourself*
- Inspiration   *e.g. Say positive things to yourself*
- Curiosity   *e.g. Be open-minded*

- Serenity   *e.g. Don't overthink and take things too seriously*
- Generosity   *e.g. Give more to people in need*
- Partnership   *e.g. Willing to take advice from others*
- Open-minded   *e.g. Be open to the points of view of others*
- Cooperation   *e.g. Focus on teamwork*
- Simplicity   *e.g. Being drama free*

If someone develops strong moral principles/values, they tend not to need a lot of external laws! The leader values outweigh their feelings.

So, let us remember that:

- Values that we hold ourselves accountable to, create behaviors that match the value itself.
- Establishing self-discipline allows us to live up to the standards we set for ourselves and build good morals.

Now that we have a better understanding of values and how to apply them to our lives, let's continue to the next chapter and discuss in detail how to build trust and healthy relationships.

Let's take action!!

Review

Let's review some key points we have talked about in chapter five. When discovering and understanding values:

- A list of beliefs or standards, that you personally choose to follow, and apply to your lifestyle!
- We don't break the law, we break ourselves against the law.
- Consider applying the value of integrity into your life.
- Being focused on values requires self-discipline and self-control.
- Seek to love storms (adversity) like the Eagle and remember that diamonds are made under pressure. God is making a masterpiece of you!

Exercise 5.1: Take Action

Manage your school/work environment so that your interruptions are limited. Write a list of the day's activities and focus on them. A technique that worked for me is something I like to call 3 For 30.

You write down three essential things that you want to accomplish that will help you complete a goal and do it for thirty days. Put it somewhere that you can always see it.

1. _____
2. _____
3. _____

For example: you can work on creating a schedule for a specified period that you will not get on Social Media or your phone in general so that you are not distracted from important things.

Exercise 5.2 : Take Action

Recognize that you are in charge of how you respond to the world and what it throws at you. The key to dealing with any unwanted thoughts is to realize that you are ultimately in charge of whether to listen to or agree with an idea. Just because you think it or hear it doesn't mean it is true. You choose your feelings about any situation. Don't give away your power. I know it is harder said than done, but it is not too early in your young life to learn how to control those run-a-way thoughts.

I want you to ask yourself three questions when you are unsure if the emotion that you are having is wrong:

1. Is this emotion/thought building me up or tearing me down?
2. Is it getting me closer to where I want to go, or taking me further away?
3. Is it motivating me to be a good action taker, or is it blocking me with fear and self-doubt?

Exercise 5.3: Take Action

Today, start making yourself a routine and a priority. Seriously!

Start eating healthier and setting aside a specific time to exercise. Then, just do it.

Write down the things you accomplish and track your progress. I have kept a workout log, and it keeps me disciplined to practice every day and see results.

When you are feeling tired, discouraged and ready to say I am done with everything, remember that you are *core value-focused and self-disciplined* as you strive towards living a fulfilling life.

Chapter 6

Building Trust and Healthy Relationships

*"Wear the hat of **people's trust** on your head daily."*

Chaz Jackson

I genuinely believe that trust is an essential thing.

Trust can lead you to build a good relationship with yourself, as well as others if taken seriously. Without trust, there will not be any quality relationships in your life; and, without quality relationships, it is hard to live a fulfilling and productive life.

So, I want you to be honest with me, but most importantly be honest with yourself!

How is your relationship on a scale one being awful and five being amazing with...

- Your friends?
- Your siblings?
- Your parents or guardian?
- Your girlfriend or boyfriend?
- Your teachers?

Maybe you have an amazing relationship with all the above, or perhaps not. Either way, this chapter is designed to help improve your outlook on how vital building trust and quality relationships are when striving towards living, learning, and leading as you are powerfully led by God.

As mentioned in previous chapters, developing a finished mindset and holding yourself to high value will help shape your integrity to deserve trustworthy relationships. I truly believe that. I have discovered on my journey that trust is solely earned by consistency in people's lives.

I want to dive into some essential qualities that it takes to build trust and healthy relationships with our peers, family members, teammates, teachers, coaches, etc. I call it The Three "BEs"." I believe that all your relationships now and in the future mirrors who you are as an individual! How you view yourself will significantly impact how you build trust and healthy relationships. Let's work inside-out. Here are some qualities needed to build trust and healthy relationships:

Be Predictable

As mentioned earlier, trust is earned by maintaining consistency in people's lives. Investing quality time and being yourself is critical in developing a healthy relationship. So, think about someone that's honestly earned your trust; those individuals that are special to you, and have proven themselves to be reliable. Most importantly, they are always trying to get to know you better, not out of curiosity, but to help or serve you more effectively. They are predictable, in my opinion.

Let's think about that one restaurant that you go to after school, or with your family and friends on the weekend. The restaurant has your favorite dish that tastes amazing each time. It can be a day where you feel like nothing is going right, and you can always depend on that one place to make your meal so perfect that you won't even think about the tough time you're having.

I have a place like that! A Chinese restaurant called Tokyo Express here in Asheville NC. Their General Tso's Chicken is amazing every time I get it. I mean, AMAZING! The golden crust on the chicken, shrimp sauce, rice, and sweet carrots are always cooked to perfection. It always hits the spot. To me, they are predictable because I can count on them to deliver a quality meal when I need their services.

71

Another example would be the Statue of Liberty located in New York. Regardless of the number of people standing outside observing the statue, if it is raining, snowing, night or day, the statue does not change! It is in the same position 86,400 seconds a day. Now, I am not giving this example to advise you to act like a statue physically and stand weirdly in the school hall every day at 1:30pm. I just honestly believe that the symbolic characteristics of a statue, such as building good moral values and confidence throughout your journey can be applied to our everyday lives as we continue to develop trustworthy habits throughout our experiences in high school, college, and the real world.

Consider characteristics such as:

1. Being exactly where you're expected to be, or say you're going to be.
2. Honoring promises you make to people.
3. Doing what you say and live by example.
4. Being consistent and dependable.
5. Showing integrity.

Be Sincere

Building trust and healthy relationships require you to be honest. There will be some situations in life, where you may feel that telling the whole truth could potentially make circumstances harder than they need to be. But, I would say 10 out of 10 times, honesty will give relationships a longer lasting chance of survival. When you take pride in being sincere, you show the other individual that you care about them. Also, I believe it is worth mentioning that when you take an interest in listening to your parents, friends, and teachers, they could potentially provide valuable information you can use to create value for yourself.

I personally believe with all my heart if you wear the hat of people's trust on your heads daily, it will set us up for a sincerer approach to life's circumstances. I try to be truthful and honest because I care about you. *I wear your trust on my head because it keeps me looking at the bigger picture of my life.* My greatest achievements or pains are not even about me anymore. They are about something higher than me and serve for a greater purpose. It is about leaving a fruitful legacy. I take pride in living, learning, and leading as I am powerfully led by God.

I know this might sound weird what I am about to share, but it works for me, and I genuinely believe it can work for you as well.

I imagine having an invisible hat on my head. The faces of people in my life are on the hat. For example, my wife's face and my daughter's face (wife is pregnant as I write this chapter). There are the faces of the people I mentor and fellowship with at Church or in the community. The many faces I see when I am up on stage speaking at schools, conferences, and community events. These are the faces of people that look up to me, and sincerely trust me to make the best decisions for our relationship and myself personally.

For example, if I get the urge to drink, I think about the faces on my invisible hat. If I think about surfing on the internet and viewing unhealthy stuff, like porn, I think about the faces on my invisible hat. I think about how my actions would impact that individual that I am helping overcome the habit. When I think like that, the urge leaves me. If I think about making a wrong decision at work, that could affect my job status, I remember the invisible hat. I consider all those people that trust me to make the right choices and I stay away from that bad urge. Keeping those faces in my mind, knowing that if I get out of character, making a contrary life-changing decision can ruin everything I am building for God's Kingdom.

Wearing the hat of people's trust on my head daily is the best decision I ever made for myself, and my family's sake. It has made me sincere!

I challenge you to use this problem-solving tool to help you in everyday life decisions.

Other characteristics that relate to being sincere are:

1. If you do lie, come clean asap
2. Speak from the heart, people will notice
3. Express your feelings in a healthy way
4. Keep secrets others are open to sharing with you

Be Exposed

I challenge you to expose who you are to people you like and trust!

Now, I am not referring to showing any flesh, let's keep it PG folks! I am referring to actually expressing your real thoughts and feelings to others. I also challenge you to try to get to know new people and to get to know the people in your life now better. You will be able to serve them better. You will be surprised at how much more your relationships will grow healthier, physically, and mentally.

The bible speaks about boasting or clearly speaking about your weaknesses. It is your faith in the Creator that allows you to feel at ease speaking of your struggles and imperfections. You have hope that He will provide solutions for you.

There is power in thinking this way.

I am sure you are like, you're crazy Chaz, *I am not sharing my weaknesses. No one at school or in my neighborhood is getting the upper hand on me.*

Pump your breaks and hear me out.

I have discovered on my journey that when you find the power to share your authentic thoughts to people, whether good or bad, is a significant step in building trust and healthy relationships. I invite you to remember a quote I shared earlier in the book by Lecrae,

"Don't be afraid of your scars, they prove to wounded people that healing is real."

I believe that scars are thoughts that are holding you back from being your true self.

Scars can be waking up in a bad mood in the morning, to feeling depressed because you personally think no one cares about you. Or, a tragic event such as losing a loved one, or domestic violence that you have overcome, and you think you can help someone else by showing you can relate to what they are going through. **When you share meaningful thoughts with others, the power it holds on you decreases, and you begin to build ways of overcoming them.** This is the correct definition of "Be Exposed."

Growing up, I used to think I was the only person that had my problems. I believed the world was against me at times and no one truly understood me. I was right, no one really understood me. I held everything inside all the time. Substance abuse and bad behavior were commonplace in my life as a way of masking my feelings.

I was 25 years old when I really began to *open up* and deal with my authentic thoughts and feelings. It was the best decision I ever made. I look back and wish I discovered this sooner in life. That is why I want to make you aware of this in a passionate way. Learn to be ok with asking questions, sharing, and learning ways to deal with your perceptions, thoughts, and feelings.

When you expose the things that keep you from being real in front of your friends such as fear, guilt, and shame (what I like to call the FGS Syndrome), you allow yourself to work towards your most durable version of yourself. You nurture self-esteem, and potential growth. There is limited room for depression, anxiety, low self-worth. It is also worth mentioning that you realize that there are others that are going through similar circumstances, and you are not alone! **Exposing your weaknesses is an action of a real leader.**

Other characteristics worth mentioning:

1. When presented with a question, such as "How are you doing"? Don't just say "I'm fine," or "I'm ok," but open yourself up. Consider a response like: "I am ok, but I am really nervous about today's test, hope I do well," or "I been upset because my brother has not been doing well lately."
2. Admit if you are not willing to share
3. Maintain self-control
4. Remember that sharing life and getting feedback is just information. What others say about you don't really matter. How you feel about yourself is what truly matters! I know that is easier said than done. You must learn not to take things so personally. Just welcome comments and use what helps you. Honestly, be willing just to say, *thanks for caring enough to listen, telling me what you see, and let me know how you personally feel.*

I hope the 3 "BEs" concept makes sense to you. I think it is worth mentioning that things are not accomplished overnight. Building trust and healthy relationships take investing time and energy in your personal growth as well as others. You are on a right path by reading this book, by the way! Take things one day at a time and remember to be yourself to your best ability. Also, not every interaction needs to be severe or personal. Sometimes a lack of time or the situation just doesn't allow it.

Empowering Yourself and Others

One of the greatest gifts you can give anyone when building trust and healthy relationships are working towards empowering yourself, by empowering others and showing love while doing it. Think about it, what is more fulfilling than helping those you truly care about overcome difficulties and investing time in them to see their goals come true? By doing this, you will feel more fulfilled, and your actions will begin to create a legacy that inspires others. Also, here is another benefit: the more you help other people succeed in life, the more they will want to help you succeed. Most successful people are ALWAYS successful in what they go after because they have helped so many people get what they want.

You are never too young to start applying this principle. People naturally support those who have supported them. The same will be right for you. A wise spiritual leader once taught me to be a student to those above me, a teacher to those below me, and a fellow helpmate to those on the same level. Apply this to your life. It is good advice for all of us.

Some examples on how to empower yourself by empowering others:

- Help a classmate study in a subject they are struggling in.
- Help someone who is being bullied.
- Help a neighbor around the yard.
- Stay after practice to help a teammate understand and learn the playbook better.
- Be willing to work in groups vs. alone all the time
- Speak up and give your opinions in conversations.

I truly believe you are taking a huge step forward reading this chapter. I am so excited thinking about, how awesome of a friend you are becoming. Consider this affirmation below that I say to myself daily, that's helping me build trust and healthy relationships:

I am surrounded around friends who have done what I want to do and done it authentically. They have a positive attitude, solution-oriented approach to life, and strives to accomplish their dreams and goals, regardless of the circumstance.

You just took another huge step forward reading this chapter. I truly believe that! Let's move on to the next chapter, and gain clarity on building confidence and quality I like to call successful worthiness.

Review

Let's review some key points we have talked about in chapter six.

- Trust is an essential factor that can lead you to build a good relationship with yourself, as well as others if taken seriously.
- All your relationships now and in the future mirror who you are as an individual.
- Be predictable
- Be sincere
- Be exposed
- Wear the hat of people's trust on your head when making decisions for your life.
- People naturally support those who have helped them.

Exercise 6: Take Action

1) When someone asks you how you are doing, instead of saying "I'm good," take the time to share your actual thoughts with that person.

2) List three people that you would like to trust and have a healthy relationship with. Do they show the qualities of the three BEs? How can you apply the concepts to your life proactively?

    1. _____

    2. _____

    3. _____

3) If you find it hard to be open up to people, create a list of things that you feel are keeping you from sharing your authentic thoughts (write down everything that comes to mind). I challenge you to share at least one thing with someone and see how it affects you.

Chapter 7

Successful Worthiness

"When there is no enemy within, the enemy outside can do you no harm."

African Proverb

You are so unique and rare! Our Creator was particular when He made you.

I scream this at the top of my lungs with joy to tell you this. You are worthy of everything you can imagine!

Will things be tough, YES! Everything worth having will have difficult stages. Never let anyone tell you it cannot be done because, IT CAN!

I want to share a story with you about a father and daughter.

The father was a successful laundry mat owner that loved his seventeen-year-old daughter very dearly. One night while the father was sitting in his chair, the daughter walked up to him very slowly with a confused look on her face. She asked him,

"Father, what is my worth?"

The father stared at his daughter for a few seconds. Then, he stood up, walked towards a small safe a few feet from his chair and pulled out a ring with a colorful stone. He said to her,

"Before I answer this question, I want you to do me a favor. In the morning, I want you to take this ring here to the street corner

Downtown. See how much you can get for it, but I don't want you to sell it!"

She said "Ok, Father," and he gave a ring to his daughter.

The next day she woke up, bright and early and took the ring to the street corner Downtown. When she returned later that afternoon, she told her father that the most anyone wanted to pay for the stone was three dollars!

The daughter said, "I honestly didn't think it was worth that much."

The father smiled at his daughter and said,

"I want you to take the ring to the Jewelry Market tomorrow and see what you can get, but don't sell it."

The daughter looked at her father puzzled, but she did what he asked the next day. said okay. When she returned later that day, she rushed into the house, and said,

"Father, someone offered us three hundred dollars for the ring, can we sell it now?"

Her Father told her that he wanted her to take it to another place tomorrow. He asked her to go to the jewelry museum a few miles outside of the city. The daughter agreed to it. Like the other two times, she woke up bright and early and went to the jewelry museum.

She returned home that afternoon full of joy! She said to her father,

"There was someone at the museum that's willing to buy the ring for 3 million dollars, can we please sell it now?"

The father was amused by his daughter's excitement and asked her to sit down beside him. The father said,

"This is the exact ring that you took to the street corner Downtown, right?"

His daughter nodded her head in agreement. He looked his daughter in the eyes, and asked,

"What do you think the difference is?"

The daughter thought about the question for a minute, and answered,

"Maybe they can see something in the ring that others cannot see, Father."

The father stated with happiness, "Now you are starting to get it."

The father went on to explain to his daughter that worth is based on where you are in most cases and how you view yourself. If someone or something is not giving you what you deserve, then you are in the wrong place.

I personally believe we all can relate to the ring in this story. We must pay attention to the toxic environments that limit our worthiness. A toxic environment is a place or situation that causes you repeated negative feelings and doesn't support your growth physically or mentally in a positive way.

Some examples of toxic environments could be:

1. Unhealthy relationships.
2. Situations where substance abuse is prevalent.
3. Where your safety is in question (being abused, bullied, life in danger, etc.)
4. Not growing as a person physically or mentally.
5. Not able to be yourself (acting like someone else)

When we think of feeling unworthy of certain things or situations, this mindset creates some of the following:

1. Not understanding who you truly are.
2. Behaving out of character or in unhealthy ways.
3. Feeling a lack of confidence and having low self-esteem.
4. Thinking negative thoughts like "I'm not up for the task,"" I'm not good enough," "I am not at my best."
5. Feeling physically tense, shaky, or sluggish in old and new environments.

You must be careful of toxic situations and how you personally see and speak to yourself. At times, your environment can be out of your own control, such as the public school you have to attend, or staying with parents that don't make the best decisions. I encourage you to realize that regardless of how bad your environment or circumstances are, you can still learn to develop positive perspectives, thoughts, and feelings about yourself and others in general.

You are built by our Creator to succeed! Remember the finished mindset discussed in Chapter One? Regardless of your culture, school, or living circumstances you should always strive to put yourself in a position to have successful worthiness. Greatness created you, therefore greatness is always inside you. I encourage you never to let anyone make you feel that you are not smart enough, pretty enough, or confident enough to go after your goals and dreams.

You are the author of your life story!

You can live a fulfilled life. You must create and nurture the habit of believing you deserve to be happy.

Let's take a look at four attributes that I believe are useful in helping feel successful worthiness and along with critical tips on living, learning and leading powerfully:

Belief

If you believe in your ability to accomplish your dream, your success and feelings of worthiness will follow. The most important person who needs to believe in your dreams and gifts is…

YOU!

As a leader, you must believe more than anyone else in the world. There is a high chance that when you express your dreams and goals to others, you could be made fun of, looked down on, or someone could just come straight out and say "*you cannot do it.*" You cannot give people the satisfaction of predicting your life. It is encouraging to learn from everyone, but at the end of the day, you are in control 100%. There are tons of success stories where the only person who believed their dreams and goals was possible was the person going after the goal. You have to learn to be your own biggest fan!

Clarity

When you have a clearly defined goal and strategy behind what you want, success will follow. Your clarity about what your goal is, and your recognition of the positive outcome will create success. Whatever your goal is, remember that the world is full of time and energy theft constantly trying to steal your attention. Get a clear and focus picture in your head, use external affirmations to assist you in being laser-focused.

Examples are a motivational screensaver on your computer that you see every day, or a vision board you keep handy.

Organization

Having a well-organized plan is vital when working your way through the sometimes-complicated process of success.

It is so easy for us to get distracted in this world we live in. I know it is easier said than done, but you must get in the habit of writing things down to be an effective leader. A well thought out, organized step-by-step plan will aid you in building successful worthiness. I also truly believe writing things down on paper makes the goal feel real and keeps you laser-focused. A goal without an action plan, in my opinion, is just a daydream. People striving toward successful worthiness write things down!

Here is an example of a goal setting sheet below. Since I love the sport of football and played linebacker, I call it the: 30-Day Tackle.

Why is this achievement so important to you? Be specific!

1.

2.

3.

Biggest Difficulties/Challenges

1.

2.

3.

30-Day Tackle (accomplishment)

1.
2.
3.

What three things would you like to accomplish that would put you on the right path to achieving your 30-day goal or goals in the next 7 days?

1.
2.
3.

Support

Who you hang around is essential when on the journey of being successful. If you surround yourself with supportive and positive people, you will more likely be motivated to make confident decisions towards your goals. Your support team will have a major impact on the way you think, speak and act. You must be picky about who you let in your circle. Remember, you need to try to limit the toxic environment. If you have a negative influence on your life, it is vital to protect yourself and your dream, so if necessary, remove them. Removing negative energy that's not serving you creates new space in your life that is positive and necessary when building successful worthiness. In other words, your authentic you!

I hope all of this makes sense. I want to continue this chapter with what I like to call the worth-building list.

I encourage you if you struggle with feeling worthy, lack confidence or self-esteem to look at these valuable terms below and use them as affirmations on a healthy and rewarding basis. I personally believe **positive self-talk** is an excellent tool to invent new thoughts and create healthy habits that build self-worth. Building self-worth and esteem takes time and a good amount of effort. Remember, things don't happen overnight. Yes, I cannot say this enough: you are worthy of greatness, but you must proactively remind yourself of what you want.

Repetition is the golden key!

Use good images and pictures in your mind of where you want to be and what it takes to get it daily.

Repeat and repeat daily, and take action on applying this to your life.

Now, I am not saying you must memorize all of these, instead, use the ones that serve you the best. Also, add to this list your own affirmations. I challenge you to speak the life you want into existence. *Taking action creates truth!*

This makes me so excited to think about. Remind yourself daily who you are, and what you are striving for. Remember you are your biggest fan! Know your worth!

Self-Worth Building List

1. Acceptance: *I feel accepted by my peers.*
2. Achievement: *I have achieved what I set out to.*
3. Ambition: *I always strive to better myself.*
4. Attractiveness: *I will look after my personal appearance.*
5. Caring: *I always take the feelings and circumstances of other people into consideration.*
6. Compassion: *I show concern for others and myself.*
7. Confidence: *I am faithful in my own skills and abilities.*
8. Courtesy: *I am polite and considerate of others.*
9. Creativity: *I have original ideas.*
10. Dependability: *I am reliable and trustworthy.*
11. Fairness: *I am fair to myself and to others.*
12. Family: *I have a happy and loving family.*
13. Flexibility: *I can adjust to new or unusual situations easily.*
14. Friendliness: *I have close and supportive friends, and I am considered a good friend to others.*
15. Fun: *I am considered good company and take time out to enjoy myself.*
16. Generosity: *I am willing to give and not always take.*
17. Health: *I am physically well and healthy.*

18. Honesty: *I am truthful and genuine.*
19. Humility: *I am not always self-promoting.*
20. Humor: *I am always looking for opportunities to make myself and others laugh.*
21. Independence: *I trust myself and make the right decisions.*
22. Justice: *I am equal and fair to others.*
23. Knowledge: *I will not stop learning.*
24. Love: *I am loved by those close to me and around me.*
25. Loyalty: *I am reliable and trustworthy.*
26. Popularity: *I am well liked by many people.*
27. Power: *I have control over my life and others.*
28. Realism: *I see things realistically.*
29. Respect: *I have people who trust and look up to me, and I do the same to others.*
30. Responsibility: *I make healthy decisions to my best ability and knowledge.*
31. Risk: *I am willing to take healthy risks and make the most of the opportunities that come my way.*
32. Safety: *I am safe and secure in what I think and what I do.*
33. Self-Control: *I am disciplined and govern my own actions.*
34. Self-esteem: *I love myself, just as I am.*
35. Self-knowledge: *I have a deep, honest understanding of myself.*
36. Spirituality: *I am growing spiritually with God.*
37. Strength: *I am physically and mentally strong.*
38. Success: *I am willing to strive towards achieving everything I set out to, or at least give it a try.*
39. Tolerance: *I accept and respect those different from me.*
40. Virtue: *I live an ethical and moral life.*
41. Wealth: *I am wealthy and prosperous.*

Bruce Lee once said,

"Always be yourself and have faith in yourself, do not go out and look for a successful personality and try to duplicate it."

I encourage you to be yourself.

I believe working toward something you really want to will play a key role in building your successful inner worthiness. Making goals will give your life meaning and make you feel fulfilled. Acknowledging daily that you deserve an environment that helps you succeed, will motivate you to be who you are destined to be. The successful person you are born to be!

Now that you understand ways to build your self-esteem and maintain the feeling of worthiness, let's go to the next chapter and discuss how to fuel your light of inspiration!

Review

Let's review some key points we have talked about in chapter seven on successful worthiness:

- You must pay attention to the toxic environments that limit your worthiness.
- You honestly must build the habit of believing you deserve to be happy.
- Belief helps you build confidence.
- Clarity helps you build confidence.
- Organization helps you build confidence.
- Support helps you build confidence.
- Be proactive in creating a successful self-worth building list to assist you in achieving success in your life.

Exercise 7: Taking Action

1) Take the time today to write down on an index card your top five self-worth building terms. Practice each day memorizing (at least three times) the phrases or creating your own that work for you. Build a goal for the next 21 days to hold yourself accountable to a specific date starting out! Even if you are not, at this moment completely visualizing what the phrases are saying, remember repetitive thoughts become a reality eventually.

Everything begins with an idea. You become what you think about!

e.g.

- Spirituality: I am growing spiritually with God.
- Caring: I always take the feelings and circumstances of other people into consideration.
- Confidence: I am faithful in my own skills and abilities.
- Self-Control: I am disciplined and govern my own actions.
- Wealth: I am wealthy and prosperous.

Chapter 8

Fuel the Light of Inspiration

"People are like stained-glass windows. They sparkle and shine when the sun is out, but when the darkness sets in, their true beauty is revealed only if there is a light from within."

Elisabeth Kubler-Ross

1) What do you believe are your roles as a student that inspire others?
2) Do you seek and apply the advice of parents and elders?
3) If your parents are not around, do you have a mentor or someone you can talk to for guidance?
4) Are you walking towards greatness?
5) Will you choose today to take ownership of your own inspiration and success?

I dare you to take the questions above seriously and think about who you are an inspiration too. Inspiration defined from my point of view is finding ways to energize, motivate, and create a sense of direction for yourself. This positive energy in turn serves as motivation and inspiration to others. I also want you to think about who is inspiring and influencing you right now!

So, stop reading this book right now, and check the last five text messages in your phone. Were the messages inspiring? Look up, turn your head from side to side, and pay attention to the people around you. Are they encouraging?

When I think about the questions above, it brings back a memory of personal inspiration. It takes me back to East Rutherford High School in 2004. Our 4x100 meter boys relay team in my junior year in school was made up of four boys. My cousin Scottie was the first leg, I was the second, Isaiah was the third, and my other cousin Brandon was the last leg, or "the finisher." This team was made up of a family that genuinely inspired each other to give it our all. I remember we always encouraged each other to hold the vision of making it to the Highschool 2A Track and Field Championship, held at North Carolina State University. We would stay later after track practice to work on our mechanics with the handoffs. We all urged Scottie to work on coming out of the blocks as quickly as possible, since he was the race starter for us. We encouraged Brandon to stay focused and finish strong for us.

I remember going to Regionals at Appalachian State University and feeling nervous going up against one of the 2A top contenders at the 4 X 100-meter dash. I knew if we were not able to keep up with them, it would put our team in a tight spot. This team was standing in our way of achieving the State Championship. I remember my cousin Brandon pulling me to the side and saying,

"Just do the best you can, Chaz. I am always going to have your back. You are the best at what you do. Go out and prove it."

That inspiration was much needed at that moment because he made me believe more in myself. This inspiration took hold of the entire team. I can remember warming up on the turf field, already sweating as it was around 85 degrees. As we went to set-up for the race, I watched Scottie positioning himself in the blocks. I remember there being a total of five teams in the race. I began looking around, holding the gaze of my opponents with my heart pounding a million beats a minute.

Then, "POW!", the gun went off. Scottie got a fantastic jump out of the blocks. He was neck to neck with an opponent coming around the corner. I was saying to myself,

"Don't drop the baton Scottie, don't drop the baton Chaz. If you drop the baton, you will lose the race".

Scottie was approaching, and I began to take off in my lane. We had developed a cadence of saying "stick" at the exchange. I remember Scottie saying "Stick!", and automatically I reached back, received baton, and took off like a bullet. I didn't look at anyone, I was laser-focused looking towards Isaiah. I ran as fast as I possibly could. You would have thought the biggest dog in the world was chasing me and was inches away from my gluteus maximus! I was neck to neck with the best and handed the baton off to Isaiah! I allowed my anxiousness and fear to be the fuel for my engine. My team's inspiration carried us to winning Regionals and being selected to go to the State Championship at North Carolina State University that year. This was one of the best experiences I had during my high school career. We didn't win at State, but again, what an experience!

I believe this story is a good illustration of inspiration because we took pride in serving each other and wanting the best outcome for the whole team. Watching those guys give it their all and leaving it all on the track inspired me to be a better teammate. It is amazing after all these years that those group of guys are still in my heart and impacting me positively to this day.

As you can see, who you spend your time around is a significant puzzle piece when creating a picture of what being inspired, or inspiring others means.

So, I challenge you to pay attention to who is "fueling your light!"

What is this light I am referring to?

From my point of view, led by God, it is your inner knowledge, beauty, love, joy, faithfulness, and excitement to put forth effort towards your passions, dreams, and goals. This light is the ideas that you are eager to share with the world. Who is inspiring you, promoting and fueling your light? It is great agony, or in other words sad and depressing if your inner light is blown out in my opinion.

I want to give some examples to be self-aware of regarding how to recognize who is fueling your light, and who is trying to blow out your light of inspiration.

Examples of individuals who are fueling your light:

1. Persons who have energized presence. *e.g. you can be in the worst mood, and when they come around, you start to feel uplifted and better about yourself.*

2. Persons who are a good influence: *e.g. they fuel your light by encouraging you to read positive books, magazines, and/or listen to music that promotes a positive or uplifting message.*

3. Persons who provide constructive criticism: *e.g. Imagine a scenario you had an argument with your ex-girlfriend at the movies. This kind of person will have no problem "calling you out" and letting you know that you were wrong for speaking to her that way. They eventually fuel your light by expecting better from you.*

4. Persons who nourish your soul: *e.g. when you were having a tough time seeing your parents go through a divorce, these individuals fuel your light by showing they care, and are willing to tend to your needs. They look to encourage during adversity.*

5. Believers and Supporters: *e.g. the times you were struggling with learning math problems in geometry class, these individuals did not hesitate to help you. They fuel your light by reminding you that you can pass the upcoming exam.*

Some ways that can help you stay inspired (fuel your light) and attract like-minded people are:

- Strive to be successful daily. Determined people are inspiring.
- Create a clear vision (mentioned in chapter 4) of your life of success and keep that vision front and center daily.
- Understand and honor your core values. All actions should serve your values in life.
- Develop and sustain a healthy lifestyle (exercise, eating healthy, etc.).
- Don't procrastinate. Do not fall into the fear trap that will keep you down.
- Believe in yourself during adversity.
- Define your goal and supporting strategies so that you have a clear direction.

- Take pride in serving others in an area of gifting by maintaining a finished mindset.
- Be caring and compassionate.

Examples of individuals who are trying to **blow out your light:**

1. They want you to live according to their dreams: *e.g. they blow out your light expecting you to act in consideration to the things they are interested. They don't expect nor respect an opinion from you.*
2. They cause fear, guilt, and shame: *e.g. continually blowing out your light by using words that tear you down physically, emotionally, and mentally.*
3. They constantly bring up your painful past: *e.g. they're always reminding you of the mistakes you have made in the past and won't let you recover and grow from them.*
4. They hold you back: *e.g. they blow out your light by taking up time with meaningless behavior and actions, distracting you from your dreams.*
5. They can be backstabbers: *e.g. they will wish you well to your face, while secretly hoping you would fail and speaking negatively of you to others. When you find out about their actions, it blows out your light and limits your inspiration.*
6. They take advantage of you: *e.g. they will manipulate you into doing what they want, whenever they want.*
7. They try to make you more like them and less like yourself: *e.g. they try to make the decisions about where you go to college, your major and where you will work after school.*
8. They pressure you to make negative choices: *e.g. they will try to talk you into doing things like skipping out on a restaurant bill thinking it would be funny and exciting.*
9. Complaining, Whining, Nagging, and Gossiping People: *e.g. they look forward to talking about the girl in English class, or they're quick to flip out on you for things that weren't your fault.*

Some ways that will help you deal with individuals who are blowing out your light:

- Talk to them about it: Organize a time to speak face to face, not through text message, social media, etc.! I say this because you cannot read tone through words. Things can get taken the wrong *easily (I know this is easier said than done but try for me.)*

- Challenge them to accept responsibility for their actions. I also challenge you to tell them how they are not inspiring or helping you to encourage others.

- Explain calmly why you feel upset by their behavior and how it is affecting your mood and relationship with them.

- Ask someone you like and trust for their opinion about the situation. Hearing another idea could possibly help you make the right decisions.

- Once you have told your side of the story, leave it up to them to make the next move. To be honest, you are probably better off without someone that's not fueling your light or inspiring you to succeed. Again, what I am sharing is hard to hear and easier said than done. I know from experience some of the closest people to you don't have your best interest at hand. Yet, unless they acknowledge what they've been doing, then it's not going to stop.

I challenge you to hold yourself to value. A toxic friend is not a friend at all.

As always, I want to encourage you to talk about these chapters with people you like and trust. It brings out the best in you and them.

Make a commitment to fuel the light of others. Try to appreciate something about every person you interact with. Make a commitment to tell the truth, as best you can, in all conversations. Commit to doing it for 1 day, then 2 days in a row, the 7 days. If you find that you didn't succeed at the goal you set, just start over! Be willing to start over as many times as it takes.

Build that muscle of habit physically and mentally. Learn to enjoy the moments of uplifting and fueling the light of someone in a small way. Notice how it makes you feel when you do that.

I want to dive even deeper into the next chapter as we talk about 12 roles that you will without a shadow of a doubt, experience throughout your life. I want you to learn about them, prepare yourself and discover problem-solving techniques to overcome them when necessary.

Review

Let's review some key points we have talked about in chapter eight on fueling the light of inspiration:

- Inspiration defined from my point of view is finding ways to energize, motivate and create a sense of direction for yourself which will in return motivate others.
- Be self-aware of who is fueling your light, as well as who is blowing out your light.
- Allow the adversity or difficulties you face to be an educational experience for you to grow physically and mentally.

Exercise 8: Taking Action

1) Look at your top five text messages and write down the tone of conversations on paper. Was the talk inspiring? Is that person inspiring you to be a better you?

_____

_____

_____

_____

2) Write down the top ten people that are influencing your life right now. Are they fueling or blowing out your light? Let's make some healthy changes, right now!

1.

2.

3.

4.

5.

6.

7.

8.

9.

10.

Remember, accepting yourself for who you are flaws and all, will make you feel more inspired. You will be motivated to inspire others.

Chapter 9

Know Your Roles

"It is easier to build strong children than to repair broken men."

Fredrick Douglas

I am super excited about this chapter.

I challenge you to be laser-focused and open-minded to learning about yourself on a deeper level. I am proud to provide, 12 roles that you will experience in some way, without a doubt during your time here on this planet. I feel it is essential to make you aware of masks that you can wear in life!

This book has been written and published to assist you in overcoming the adversity these roles can create. I want to equip you with problem-solving tools that can help you with overcoming adverse circumstances and behaviors as they can limit you from living, learning, and leading powerfully.

I want to provide tools I've learned from Biblical studies, personal life experiences, and other sources that has impacted my life positively. I want to share based on what I've learned from negative behaviors/roles that can be limiting, and how you can make them an inspiration for yourself and others.

Remember, this could be tough to deal with because I am challenging you to evaluate your own personal behaviors, as well as the behaviors of close friends and family members that influence you.

Take this challenge with me and learn about yourself.

I encourage you to read each role, spend some time going over it, and see if you notice and can personally relate to any of the characteristics, thoughts, and/or feelings. Also, don't be afraid to set up group discussions for each one!

You will look at three problem-solving techniques that can help you overcome the negative aspects of the roles and helping us become greater versions of ourselves.

You will practice these three problem-solving skills:

1. Understanding - *Build focus and self-awareness of your thoughts and feelings and how they affect yourself and others. This will help you overcome unwanted behaviors.*
2. Taking Action- *Focus on changing behaviors and learning ways to be a better and productive individual.*
3. Tracking Progress - *Find opportunities to work on problems and always track how far you have come in making the right decisions (goal setting).*

Again, you will read the scenarios below, and use the three problem-solving tools, to build ways to overcome. Also, don't be so hard on yourself when viewing these and noticing any kind of negative behaviors in your life. Believe me, we all have them.

Practicing good habits builds good habits.

For example, if you only dribble a basketball with your right hand, it would be pretty tough to dribble or drive for a layup with your left hand. You must practice dribbling with your left hand until it becomes natural and comfortable.

The concept is the same with building behaviors and overcoming the roles I am about to share. I provided a brief thought and action taker at the end of each. Also, continue seeking out your parents, mentors, or other role models that you like and trust. Talk about these scenarios with them and discuss healthy ways to overcome behaviors that are keeping you from being successful.

Talk about how they make you feel. Get as much feedback as you can. Never think there is only one way to solve a problem. There are multiple ways to overcome a circumstance; the key is finding what works best for you.

My ultimate goal is to make you aware of the roles and behaviors they carry and get you thinking about how they can limit you from living, leading, and learning powerfully!

So, let's get started!

Victim Role

Tommy believes he is a victim in every situation. He blames others for his life circumstances and his feelings. He always has sad stories to share, without any plan for changing the outcomes. Tommy is rarely positive in school or at home. He believes if he does something wrong (makes bad grades, is violent toward others, etc.,) he can shift the blame. For example, he might blame his actions on his father not being around, or his mother having to work two jobs to support the family. He is always pointing the finger at others for his behavior. Tommy believes if he sticks with a story long enough whether he is right or wrong, he will not be held accountable for his feelings or actions.

Understanding - learn to take responsibility for your own behaviors and use your unwanted or harmful situations as opportunities to grow your character. Let your story be your testimony!

Taking Action - say something positive about yourself and others on a daily basis.

Tracking Progress - keep track of how many situations you was wrong, and you took full resposibility for 21 days.

Notes

1) _____

_____

_____

_____

2) _____

_____

_____

_____

3) _____

_____

_____

_____

Not Fair Role

Heather repeatedly thinks life is just "not fair." For example, she believes it is not fair having to live in a group home. When challenging things to happen to her, such as people holding her accountable to doing her chores at the group home, or being more organized with her school work, she doesn't think it is worth the effort. She believes the rules in life do not apply to her. For example, if she was to miss the due date of homework and her teacher or guardians punish her for it, she will act out and become angry. She does not like to be held accountable for anything!

Understanding - Realize to be successful in life you must hold ourselves to a personal standard. The things you care about must outweigh your temporary feelings. Take the time to understand why it is important to your parents, teachers, guardians, etc., that you succeed at the task he/she is requesting.

Taking Action - Listen to the other person's side of the story and see if it is a suggestion that can contribute to your success as a person.

Tracking Progress- Keep a record on paper for 21 days of how many times you say "it's not fair" or find yourself being in a position of feeling used, or not treated in the right way. Is the comment promoting your success?

Notes

1) _____

_____

_____

_____

2) _____

_____

_____

_____

3) _____

_____

_____

_____

Unique Role

Kim thinks the world just doesn't understand her issues. For example, she has the thoughts of not feeling pretty enough at school. She believes her thoughts and feelings are rare and no one else can relate to her. Because she finds others cannot truly understand her, she thinks she shouldn't have the same responsibilities as them, for example, splitting and completing chores with a sibling or dealing with all the school requirements like her classmates. Kim thinks she should be held to a different set of rules and regulations than others. She doesn't really care about the feelings of others. She is also very impolite and inconsiderate. She only focuses on and cares about her own opinions and protects them at all costs.

Understanding - We all have different walks of life, and no one is perfect. Don't be afraid of who you are.

Taking Action - Find someone you like and trust and share your thoughts. When you talk about your negative thoughts and feelings, they lose their control and power over you.

Tracking Progress - Notice how you feel after sharing your true feelings and keep a record on when you find someone who can relate to your problem and inspire you to strive for a solution.

Notes

1) _____

_____

_____

_____

2) _____

_____

_____

_____

3) _____

_____

_____

_____

One-way Role

Zak is very protective of his boundaries and wants them to be respected at all costs. For example, he does not like his sister going into his room. However, he feels it is always okay to go and mess around in his sister's room anytime he wants. Zak doesn't like his friends to embarrass him in front of people but finds it acceptable to always makes fun of the kid that sits next to him in History class. He does whatever pleases him.

Zak can be the most helpful person in the world if things are always going the way he plans. However, if you try and interfere with anything he values or takes pride in, you will have gained an enemy.

Understanding - Other people's feelings matter. Treat others the way you want to be treated.

Taking Action - Think about what matters to you the most and what makes you happy. Approach your relationships making the effort of wanting the other person to feel that pleasure.

Tracking Progress - Keep a record for 21 days of people you helped without expecting anything back.

Notes

1) _____

_____

_____

_____

2) _____

_____

_____

_____

3) _____

_____

_____

_____

My Way or No Way Role

Gene believes if he has a relationship with you, then he is the Boss. You do things for him, and only him. For example, Gene makes all the decisions and never allows his girlfriend to pick the places they go on dates. He does not address the opinions of others in a healthy way during disagreements. He doesn't function well with people that have a different view of things. Gene likes to ask his family and friends to breaks rules for him, with no questions asked. Rules are more like obstacles or challenges to Gene, and he is always trying to figure out a way to break them. If you do not do what Gene asks or try to change what he is asking of you, he will end the relationship quickly.

Understanding - Being open-minded to other people's opinions helps you grow physically and mentally.

Taking Action - Find someone inspiring to you and allow them to make a decision and you hold up your end to following it.

Tracking Progress - Keep track of how many times you don't make a demanding remark to people you spend most of your time with. The fewer times, the more inspiring we become.

Notes

1) _____

_____

_____

_____

2) _____

_____

_____

_____

3) _____

_____

_____

_____

Negative Role

Paul is always thinking negatively. He loves to keep secrets, be alone, and takes pride in substance abuse (using drugs and drinking, etc.) He doesn't talk about his real thoughts and feelings to anyone. He takes pride and finds excitement in knowing about crime and how to overcome authority (parents, teachers, police, etc). He enjoys hanging out with people that don't expect anything from him nor do they hold him accountable. Paul builds self-esteem from negative thinking and behavior. He gets really nervous around positive role models and tries to avoid them.

Understanding - Negative thoughts create a negative world.

Taking Action - Start hanging out with people that inspire you to want more in life. Build a circle of people that want to see you succeed for good.

Tracking Progress - Write down a list of the top five people you associate with and answer the following questions: 1) Do they want to see you succeed? 2) Do they offer you sound advice during hard and confusing times? 3) Do they personally seek success for themselves?

The key is to be able to eventually say yes to all three.

Notes

1) _____

_____

_____

_____

2) _____

_____

_____

_____

3) _____

_____

_____

_____

Anger Role

Hannah believes that if she is angry and acts out in situations, she will get whatever she wants from parents, teachers, etc. For example, Hannah wanted to go and hang out with her friends, but her mother said that she couldn't. Hannah got furious at her mother and screamed and yelled until her mother just gave into her. She is willing to stay angry with anyone for as long as it takes for them to apologize or give her what she wants. She personally believes if she acts out of character, she will always be in control of the situation.

Understanding - Anger is present in my life, and it is triggering from an unwanted habit or belief about myself that I am holding on to. Anger is a feeling that will eventually go away, but my actions could potentially be remembered forever.

Taking Action - When you become angry at yourself or others, try and change your thought pattern and become self-aware of the things that person has done to bless and/or inspire you (Ex, Mother wants the best for me, or my friend always had my back in tough times). Hold on to that thought, and ask yourself, "Is it worth creating action from anger that could ruin our relationship for the long-term?"

Tracking Progress – Take note of and write down how many times you get angry on a daily basis and how you responded to the circumstances. The goal is to have fewer episodes.

Notes

1) _____

_____

_____

_____

2) _____

_____

_____

_____

3) _____

_____

_____

_____

Wishing Role

John continually wishes for good things to happen instead of taking action and doing things for himself. He truly believes that he is so powerful that he doesn't have to do work or put forth any effort to see change. He thinks life just happens and will deal with situations as they appear. John makes promises to his parents, teachers, and friends that things will be different, such as taking responsibility for doing his homework or being committed to living out family values. Still, he tries to avoid acting on it all. He doesn't like talking about it and continuously just says "things will be different." If you ask John to put forth more effort or show progress, he will get angry and try to embarrass you. He does this so that you will not try to challenge him in the future. John truly believes he will do better without changing his behavior.

Understanding - In order to see the positive change in the world you desire, you have to first become the positive change, personally.

Taking Action - Action creates truth! During the times of wishing and desiring, take a chance on going after the things you believe in and finishing the task at hand.

Tracking Progress - Write down the things that you wish will come true and notice how each makes you feel. For the ones that genuinely gives you inspiration, strive to make them a reality one step at a time.

Notes

1) _____

_____

_____

_____

2) _____

_____

_____

_____

3) _____

_____

_____

_____

Put Off Role

Sue honestly never get things done. She is known for doing half-jobs. Not finishing things don't bother her until she is confronted about them. For example, when asked by parents to complete cleaning up the kitchen and take out the trash she started an hour ago, she gets enraged and disrespectful. This is even though she decided to talk on the phone with friends as opposed to doing as she was told. Instead of taking responsibility, she argues about not doing chores. She hopes that eventually the things she is held responsible for will be put off and not talked about. Someone else will take responsibility, finally. She doesn't like being held accountable for anything.

Understanding - Unfinished activities or work creates an unfinished life. You should strive for a finished mindset and lifestyle.

Taking Action - Learn ways to take responsibility for your actions and finish the task you set for yourself. Remember new habits takes consistency to become a positive change in life.

Tracking Progress - Write down every time you finished and completed a task, regardless of what it is. You are a finisher.

Notes

1) _____

_____

_____

_____

2) _____

_____

_____

_____

3) _____

_____

_____

_____

Dishonesty Role

Jerry will admit to other's mistakes and misconduct very easily, but not his own faults. He will say yes to doing something, just to get his parents, teachers and other authority figures off his back. When sharing a story, he will rearrange the facts to make himself come out on top. For example, Jerry got in trouble for bullying someone in school. When confronted by his parents and Principal, he says things like,

"...the other kid had told lies about me, and I was only asking about it face to face."

"I wasn't trying to be a bully!"

When in fact the other kid was innocent, Jerry will do whatever it takes to come out on top and look honest to authority figures.

Understanding - My dishonesty and negative behavior limits my chances of being an inspiring person.

Taking Action - When confronted about a mistake, hold yourself accountable and tell the truth. You will respect yourself and others in a more positive way in the long-term.

Tracking Progress - Keep a record and write down how many times you told the truth. Notice how the new habit grows.

Notes

1) _____

_____

_____

_____

2) _____

_____

_____

_____

3) _____

_____

_____

_____

False Apology Role

Nell always apologizes for her actions or mistakes, but never makes any effort to change. She will argue with her parents, be disruptive in class, and tell lies about others and completing tasks. When she is called out on her faults or actions, she admits that she was wrong, even apologizes, but does not make any changes moving forward. Saying *"I'm sorry,"* is so easy for her, and she uses it to get out of indeed taking responsibility for her actions. Personally, she truly believes that it is always the other person's fault and not her own.

Understanding - I am 100% responsible for my own actions at the end of the day, not anyone else.

Taking Action - Limit saying *"I'm sorry"* and replace it with, *"I will get things done."*

Believe that you have what it takes to be inspiring and fruitful. Be the change you want to see. Take action against your unwanted habits.

Tracking Progress - Notice how many times you say "*I'm sorry*" to others and replace with "*I will get things done.*" Keep a record for 21 days of what you finished and can change moving forward.

Notes

1) _____

_____

_____

_____

2) _____

_____

_____

_____

3) _____

_____

_____

_____

Turnaround Role

Mary is always turning her own faults around on the other person. When her parents ask her why she is making bad grades, she blames it on the teacher not liking her. When she was caught shoplifting in the mall with her best friend, she told her parents and authorities that her friend persuaded her to do it. Mary finds it very easy to make others look like the bad person. Her goal is to always be the innocent one. She does not like being challenged or questioned about her behavior.

Understanding - My decisions affect others around me. I am in control of my attitude and beliefs. You control the outcome of things being positive or negative.

Taking Action - Take 100% responsibility for my own actions. At the end of the day, not anyone else can live your life for me. **Tracking Progress** - Write down the times you take full responsibility for a life-changing situation and do not blame others for the next 21 days.

Notes

1) _____

_____

_____

_____

2) _____

_____

_____

_____

3) _____

_____

_____

_____

I hope you were able to find some benefit from these roles. If you find one of these roles hard to deal with or you become angry while reading, I encourage you to not be so hard on yourself. Changing attitudes and behaviors for the long-term takes time and consistency. This book is designed to help you overcome these roles so you are in the right place. You must just have the courage to make the first step and be willing to take daily steps towards being inspiring and living the way that makes you happy.

I believe to indeed live, learn and lead powerfully, you should continue to work on being self-aware of the twelve roles and the behaviors they can create. Next chapter you will look at priorities and how they can impact your life.

Review:

- Practice Understanding - Build focus and self-awareness of your thoughts and feelings, and how they affect you and others. This will help you overcome unwanted behaviors.
- Practice Taking Action - Focus on changing behaviors and learning ways to be a better and more productive individual.
- Practice Remembering Progress - Find opportunities to work on problems and always notice how far you have come in making the right decisions (goal setting).
- As a human, allow adversity or in other words difficulties, to be an educational experience for you to grow physically and mentally (I know this is easier said than done).

As you begin to develop new habits, I challenge you to speak words that build your self-esteem and self-confidence and develop relationships and dreams towards a greater you. Speak words of positive affirmations, encouragement, appreciation, love, acceptance, possibility, and visions towards overcoming the twelve roles mentioned in this chapter. You are on the right path to becoming a strong leader for the next generation to come.

Exercise 9 - Taking Action

1. I challenge you to write down the top 4 roles that remind you of yourself. Find someone you like and trust and talk about how to overcome the role and turn the role into a healthy growth experience! Tackle these 4 questions with each individual role:

- Identify the role you can relate to and make a list of some of the beliefs that could be limiting you to the characteristics of the role.
- Based on the role and record of ideas, what things are you doing in your daily life that influence the continued behavior?
- Decide how you want to be, act, feel moving forward. What changes do you want to see and make?
- Create a turnaround statement that affirms or gives you permission to be, perform, or feel this new way.

Chapter 10

Your Priorities

"You only have 86,400 seconds in every day of your life. Yesterday is history, tomorrow is a mystery, today is my everything."

Unknown

I read a speech comparing the challenges faced by teens. The presenter said something that caught my attention:

"The challenge that teens faced 150 years ago was hard work. The challenge that teens face today is a lack of hard work."

I said to myself, *"lack of hard work, that's the most ridiculous thing I have heard in a while. Teen and young adults are all constantly doing something. You have a lot to do, and there are only 86,400 seconds (24 hours) in a day!"*

Let's think about it. You wake up in the morning, possibly must do morning chores, and then go to school. After school, you either have your sports practice or rehearsal, followed by going to your part-time job! You cannot forget about that math test and science quiz tomorrow. You must spend time with your family and text your best friend to get some life-changing advice. On top of that, you must take care of your pet, make sure your car (if driving) is working correctly, outside of your parents' help. You probably volunteer somewhere, and I know how important it is for you to keep your room clean (right!).

What are you going to do?

I have learned so far on my journey that it is all about prioritizing and managing your time, so the important things get finished. I believe that prioritizing can also help you learn to overcome your fears, guilt, and shame and be strong during hard moments life can offer at times. Priorities can be defined as tasks, projects or goals that you treat as being more important than other tasks, plans, or intentions. For example, a priority of mine is finishing this book. So, things, like watching tv, or hanging out with my friends, are not held as a high priority during my scheduled writing times. Staying on task and finishing projects promotes success. It assists in building your self-esteem, or in other words, completing things that help build your confidence.

As I was preparing for this chapter, I came across a fantastic example of someone that holds priorities to a high standard. David Hardy is an Editor (proofreads papers, etc.) for a successful magazine. He tells a story about Richard Branson, a very successful multi-billion-dollar investor. Hardy was approached by another businessman that knew Mr. Branson was a good friend of his. He wanted to know if Mr. Hardy could ask Richard Branson would accept an offer of $100,000 to speak for an hour. Mr. Hardy told him he would see what he could do. He got in contact with Mr. Branson's office, and they presented the offer. He received word back that Mr. Branson turned down $100,000. Mr. Hardy contacted the businessman with the response. The businessman didn't take no for an answer. He upped his offer to $250,000 for the hour-long presentation. This was considered a lot of money to him. Mr. Hardy resubmitted this offer to Mr. Branson's office. Once again, Mr. Branson declined.

The offer increased to a half-million dollars ($500,000.00), a private jet to and from the speaking event for just the hour of his time. Mr. Branson's office confirmed his decline again. Mr. Hardy spoke of the businessman's frustration and disbelief. He proposed calling Mr. Branson's office and finding out the exact amount it would take to get Richard Branson to come and speak. His attitude was clearly "Whatever it takes".

Richard Branson's office called him back and said: "No amount of money would matter." They went on to say, "Right now, Richard has three main priorities he is focused on, and he will only allocate his time to those three priorities and speaking for a fee is not one of them."

David Hardy said, "Now, when I told a friend of mine this story he said *Well, it's easy for Branson to say no to easy half a million dollars, but I certainly couldn't.* I promptly replied with, *that's why you are not achieving like Richard Branson.*"

He started out with nothing like the rest of us. He's gotten to where he is BECAUSE of this dedication to focus.

I chose to use this example because it demonstrates a high standard of someone putting priorities first and staying focused. To accomplish what you set out for, you must have things in order. Think about packing your suitcase for a summer vacation or cleaning out your closet (easier said than done, right?). The better organized you are, the easier things will be to find when needed. This works the same for the outcome for your life. The better you organize yourself, the more time you will save and spend on enjoyable things. For example, you will have more time for family and friends, sporting games, school, and just more time for yourself.

Let's meet who I like to call the Lady of Priorities. I believe she is an excellent example of someone who arranges and plans their life towards being successful! For starters, she is not perfect, but she holds herself accountable to integrity and lives with a finished mindset (mentioned in chapter one.) She basically has it together. She looks at everything she must do daily and then organizes accordingly. She is always planning and 95% of the time, she's on top of things. She does her homework on time and writes papers a little in advance. She is not a fan of cramming anything, because she is self-aware of the fact that it causes stress, fear, and anxiety. Those are three things she wants to avoid at all costs. She eats healthy, makes time to exercise, and knows how to adjust her day to fit in the important things.

The things that matter the most to her, for example, are her family, friends, and staying above 3.7 GPA. Keeping a balanced life is essential to her, such as taking time out for herself, and knowing there is a time to be serious and focused, and there is a time to let loose. She doesn't depend on her father to let her know when it comes to maintenance on her car, and she takes pride in changing her a tire when needed.

She knows how to say *No*, even if it seems like a great opportunity. For example, three of her good friends stopped by her house one day and wanted to go to the mall. She said with a smile "Nah, I have a history test tomorrow, so I will have to pass on going to the mall today. Let's go this weekend or something."

Her friends were upset about it, but they had to be okay with it. She is very firm in her decisions. She knows it takes courage to stand up for yourself. Resisting peer pressure appears to some as being boring, or not fun, but she has a good understanding of it. Eventually, people come to respect your decisions. *She knows that the opinions others have of you will always change, but the opinion that you have for yourself will last forever.*

I know holding ourselves to the 'Lady of Priorities' standard is easier said than done. Yet, I genuinely believe that you are capable of achieving these goals. I want to talk about three things that can help you get on the right path toward the 'Lady of Priorities' standard.

Let's check them out!

1. Limit Distractions

There are good distractions and bad distractions, right? We mostly concentrate on the bad ones. We all do it. You must be aware of how they are impacting your life and the goals you set for yourself.

Distractions can be for example:

1. A best friend keeps calling you when you are trying to study.
2. Someone is humming while they work.
3. Your neighbor is mowing the lawn.
4. Your phone is buzzing letting you know someone has just made a comment on your social media page.
5. Someone has angered you.
6. You're thinking about what's for lunch.
7. A lack of planning and just letting life happen.

As you look back at the 'Lady of Priorities', when she told her friends that she couldn't go to the mall due to her upcoming test, she didn't give in to peer pressure. She didn't allow distractions to alter her goals of making a good grade on the next test.

Some ways to limit distractions, when you begin to lose focus:

1. Schedule daily time to focus on your priorities.
2. Turn off and limit phone conversations, social media, etc. during scheduled focus times. Just hearing your phone can allow you to lose focus
3. Limit people that don't support your priorities.
4. Hang around people that share the same values and priorities as you do (likeminded association).

2. Plan Things Out

You must have a plan!

Having a plan saves you a lot of time and puts you a half a step up. I encourage you to start small. You don't have to stress about having a master plan. It doesn't matter if you have a forty-year plan or a three-hour plan. Planning gives you a foundation; something to remember if you get distracted or lose focus.

My goal for you right now is to get you thinking! You don't necessarily need to know your career path you're going to follow, or what state you are going to live in. Start with easy and achievable decisions you can make now. An example could be planning how you are going to study for next week history exam, or how you are going to save money for your upcoming senior trip.

I have discovered on my journey that a lot of successful people keep planners. I know this is easier said than done, but it gives you some advantage when tackling goals and dreams. Think about it, how easy is it showing up to school, with a plan on which classes you go to every other hour or so. It would be crazy having to wake up every morning, and not having an idea. It is hard enough for completing grade school with a plan but trying to figure it out without one is overly stressful. Finding a planner app is one of the easiest ways to get started (Trello is one.) My wife Amy is an excellent planner, and she goes old school with a planner notebook. You can easily find in nearby supply store.

Let's get laser-focused on planning!

3. Adjust and Learn from Failures

Let's be honest here: you can plan things in life, have priorities in order, and things can still not go the way you have it on paper. You are going to fail at one time or another. Everyone does. I want you to really get a good understanding of what I am about to share next!

If you go through life with the attitude that failure is wrong, you'll be too hard on yourself when things don't go your way. You will attract more failure. Most importantly, you won't learn from your mistakes. You will never grow as a person. Sometimes that fear of failure can keep you from trying at all. Those who adjust and learn from failures eventually achieve their goals.

Let's give some examples:

- Michael Jordan missed more than 9,000 shots in his career and lost more than 300 games. Twenty-six times he missed the game-winning shot. Despite the failures, he is arguably the greatest basketball player of all time and has 6 NBA Championships among other achievements.
- Bill Gates is the founder of Microsoft and one of the wealthiest businessmen in America. His first business failed.
- Harland David Sanders (aka Colonel Sanders), businessman, and founder of Kentucky Fried Chicken (KFC) pitched his chicken recipe 1,009 times before someone finally gave him a chance. KFC is one of the most popular restaurants in America today.

What all these guys have in common is they made it a priority to keep striving after what they were passionate about, regardless of how many times they failed. They made the right adjustments. These guys realized that failure can help you discover positive things about yourself and create new opportunities in your life that you never expected. Make adjustments a priority.

Priorities for College Preparation

I want to transition into talking about college preparation.

I know that college it is not for everyone, but again as always, I plan to get you thinking about different options you can take.

Going to college isn't every person's destiny, but with the way our society is designed, without some sort of trade/skill or higher education, it is harder to succeed. Most places want a Bachelor's Degree for entry-level work. There are many people work in fast food chains with degrees from colleges waiting for an opportunity to arise. Whether you decide on a community, junior, or four-year college, the following list will help get you started in the right direction.

- Factors to consider when deciding which college(s) you would want to attend.

  1. Distance from home
  2. Cost
  3. Major
  4. Scholarships offered
  5. +University vs. Community

- Apply to ALL your college selections.
  Include every place you would want to go. You'd be surprised sometimes who might accept you!
- Start saving money.
  Get or maintain some sort of part-time job (babysitting, fast food restaurant jobs, mowing lawns)
- Start applying for general and specific scholarships.
  Scholarships in the major you choose

  1. Academic scholarships

  2. Awards/Grants/Financial Aid based on family income and finances
  3. Scholarships from your place of employment
  4. Scholarships based on culture and ethnic background

Talk with Guidance Counselors at school; they know of sites and sources to find scholarships.

- Be cognizant of your GPA and ways to improve it.
  The higher the GPA, the better your chances are of getting accepted into your school of choice.
- Start to build your Résumé.
  See examples below of blank and filled out resume:

BLANK RESUME

YOUR NAME HERE
Address
City, State, Zip Code
Phone number
Email address

EDUCATION

Your Middle or High School Here   City, State

Year – present   General education or area of concentration
List the awards, clubs, and activities you are involved in.

EXPERIENCE

Company or person for whim you worked   City, State

Year – present   Your title here

- Responsibilities and accomplishments
- Responsibilities and accomplishments

Summer Year   Company or person for whom you worked

- Responsibilities and accomplishments
- Responsibilities and accomplishments

OTHER DATA

- List other accomplishments outside school and work,
- Special training, interest and hobbies.

BHS Student

1234 Main St.
Bolivar, MO 65613

Phone: 417-399-1234 (cell)
417-777-1234 (home)
Email: bhsstudent@liberatormail.org

OBJECTIVE
To be employed as a restaurant hostess

EDUCATION
Bolivar High School, Bolivar, MO
Diploma, May, 2011, GPA 4.0

WORK EXPERIENCE
Name of Bolivar Business, Bolivar, MO
Cabinet Carpentry & Installation, June-August 2008
- Installed hardware
- Built drawers
- Operated equipment such as table saw and orbital sander

BABYSITTING
Joe Smith
Childcare, June-July, 2009
- Supervised four children
- Prepared meals
- Performed general childcare duties

CLUBS AND ACTIVITIES
Future Business Leaders of America, Member, 2008-2010
- Earned first place in E-commerce at the district level
- Earned eighth place in E-commerce at the state level
- Taught fifth graders a lesson on credit for the American Enterprise Project

Student Council, Class Representative, 2008-2010
- Assisted in organizing the Bolivar High School Veteran's Day Assembly
- Served as a student worker at the Teacher's Babysitting Night
- Participated in organizing 2008 and 2009 homecoming activities

Missouri Scholars Academy, Attendee, June 2009
- Helped create a documentary film
- Attended various workshops
- Took part in community service and leadership activities

REFERENCES
Jill Smith, Bolivar High School Teacher
emailaddress@bolivarschools.org; 417-326-5228

Joe Smith, Bolivar High School Teacher
emailaddress@bolivarschools.org; 417-326-5228

Jane Smith, Bolivar High School Teacher
emailaddress@bolivarschools.org; 417-326-5228

1401 N. Hwy D
Bolivar, MO 65613

What if college is not for me?

So, let's be honest: a college education and commitment to lifelong learning is a big step towards success. However, there are a lot of successful people who have not finished or even attended college.

It is not a requirement.

Statistics show that 20% of America's Millionaires never set foot in college. There are even billionaires in America that never finished high school. Now, I am not saying this so you can go up to your parents and tell them Chaz has inspired you to drop out of high school. I don't want any crazy phone calls from furious parents.

I am sharing these statistics because you have the power to start from anywhere and create a successful life for yourself. I personally believe college can give you an advantage when it comes to discovering your passions. The college experience can also help you to build self-discipline as you progress towards the future.

On the flip side, I don't think college is the only way to succeed. I encourage you to make it a priority to invest in yourself and surround yourself with people that have your best interest, even if college is not your primary choice! I challenge you not to be afraid to follow your heart and adjust your priorities led by God.

Stay away from worrying about what others will think (parents, teachers, mentors, etc).

If having others believing in you and your dream was a requirement for success, most of us would never accomplish anything.

You don't need to base your priorities, such as your dreams, goals, and desires on the goals, aspirations, opinions, and judgments of your parents, teachers, friends, and/or co-workers. Stop worrying about what other people think about you and follow your heart led by God. All the energy you are giving to others can be spent on thinking about and doing the things that will help you achieve your goals.

Remember this last thought:

If you would go every day to a huge tree and take five swings at it with a very sharp ax, eventually, no matter how big the tree is, it will come down. The task would be complete because you made it a priority and planned to go every day to the tree and take action. Make it a priority to know that action creates truth! As you move on to the next chapter, we will talk about how parents can impact our lives.

Review:

- Priorities can be defined as tasks, projects, or goals that you treat as being more important than others tasks, projects, or goals.
- To be successful at maintaining priorities, you should strive to hold the 'Lady of Priorities' standard, by limiting distractions, taking pride in planning, and taking small steps towards short and long-term decisions.
- Adjust and learn from failures.
- College is not for everyone, but it can give you options on discovering your passions as you progress towards the future.

Exercise 10: Taking Action

1) Write out a to-do list. Don't make it challenging. You can make your list a series of things you want to do. I challenge you to write out three things (only 3) that are realistic, and you can actually do. Don't write down anything super long, because you will get to overwhelmed and shut down, and the next thing you know you are scrolling on social media and playing video games all day. Believe me, I know!

_____

_____

_____

_____

The next day when you wake up, look at your list. I want you to ask yourself this question,

"If I did only one thing on this list today, what will inspire me and others the most? What will make me feel like I accomplished something, and today was a productive day?"

Pick something and accomplish the task by noon.

For example, maybe it is cleaning up your room, or your parent's garage. Perhaps it is spending more time, gaining more knowledge about one of your hobbies. It could be preparing for a chemistry exam, or asking out that one person you been staring at every day in the school parking lot. Whatever it is, make sure you get it done (seriously   !) Don't put it off. Take 100% responsibility for making it a priority.

Completing tasks is a great way to build self-esteem. Again, you don't have to do everything on the list. Just one thing. When you lay down that night, I want you to be proud to say, "I finished this!"

Chapter 11

Parent-Child Relationship

"There is no such thing as a perfect parent, so just be a real one."

Sue Atkins

In today's world, there are so many distractions that can potentially cause the parent-child relationship to lose focus on family values and develop unhealthy communication. Things like cell phones, computers, individual thoughts, mood, and behaviors are factors that can cause a loss of focus. You may not realize how they are affecting your family relationship as a whole.

My goal is to help you paint a good picture of the type of relationship you should strive to have with your parents. I want to help you get a better idea of the adversity that comes along with parenting and assist you in developing some productive and straightforward ways can strengthen the parent-child relationship overall.

So, let's talk about, the "perfect parents."

You have heard about them, right? Keep an open mind with me, as I give a good description of them. Let's even try and imagine that these are your parents and you are describing them to a friend after school.

Here we go:

My parents are awesome. They have been married for many years, and I have never seen them mad or argue with each other. Not even once. They are the most honest and trustworthy people I know. They always admit when they are wrong. My Dad is the perfect leader for our family, and he still has the right plans in place for family trips, goals, and values. His projects never fail. When meals are prepared, Dad is always home on time, and we sit together as a family to enjoy an excellent dinner. Every night, over dinner, we share our positive and productive day.

Mom is so easy to talk to. She never gets stressed with taking care of us or household duties. She listens to me whenever I need her. She is very reliable and dependable for all my needs. Mom and Dad always knock before they enter my room (amazing!!), and never get weird around close friends, or ask crazy questions when I go on dates.

When I am stressed and don't want to talk, they just leave me alone and wait for me to respond. My parents don't compare me to other kids and allow me to express myself the way I see fit. For example, they are not picky about the way I dress, the music I listen to, or how long I stay on the phone or internet! They have some rules but are willing to hear my opinions on them and adjust them to make me happy.

My parents admit when they are wrong, and they don't dismiss my feelings as being just moody. For example, before we moved to this area, my Mom and Dad made it a priority to ask me about how I felt about moving to this county, and the selection of schools in the district. They have a college fund for me in place, and I am applying to colleges as we speak. There is not a day that goes by that I don't love them. You are going to have so much fun when you come over to my house and meet them.

Awesome parents, right? Can you relate to this scenario above?

You probably figured out half-way through the script, these parents are fake! However, I am sure that both you and your parents can relate to a lot of the positive qualities and characteristics mentioned. I can honestly say that deep down, every parent and child would love to live up to the scenario above.

But, let's be honest; life happens.

I want to do a more realistic scenario, that you could possibly also relate to, or have personally dealt with.

Once again, imagine you're telling a friend about your parents.

Here we go:

So, about my parents. They divorced when I was three years old and got remarried. I have two step parents. They try their best to be honest people, but I got broken promises and disappointed all the time. Dad just promised a week ago that we would go to lunch tomorrow, and he canceled as usual due to work. My parents don't like each other very much, and they have a hard time admitting when they are wrong to each other, including me. They try to make their relationship work for my sake I guess. My real dad tries to be a leader for his family, and include me, but it gets hard since I am not always there. My stepmother doesn't like me very much. I think it frustrates him so much that at times, he just forgets to include me altogether.

I'm not the biggest fan of having to go back and forth to my Dad's and Mom's homes all the time. Regardless of either household, meals are prepared, but we don't always sit at the table together. Most of the time we are all gathered around the tv and sometimes even eat at separate times. We rarely have serious conversations, when someone's feelings get hurt, things just get brushed under the rug, if you know what I mean. They are both really strict on me about who my friends are, what to wear, what I am doing on the internet, and they never let me make decisions for myself. Some of the things they are telling me not to do, they are doing themselves. It is really confusing. For example, Mom and Stepdad always have friends over, and really drink a lot of beer and play loud music. Yet, they tell me it is wrong to drink.

They also argue a lot! I have seen them fight physically and I get so stressed out about it. I just wish they would get along. They always forgive each other, but it still happens every other weekend. It has gotten so sorry, that I stay at my Grandma's house on occasion. I believe Mom and Dad genuinely love me, but I wish they would include me in some of the decisions they make on my behalf. I just get so angry and frustrated. Sometimes I am thinking about quitting high-school, getting a job, and moving out on my own.

Are you sure you still want to come over?

What do you think about the second scenario above? Can you relate to some of the feelings expressed and behaviors of the parents?

When I look back on my journey, I think about some of the adversity, or in other words difficulties my parents and I have endured and overcome. I would ask myself why my mother and father made certain decisions that impacted my life forever. As I looked back, I wondered where those thoughts originated from. I think about the times I didn't agree with my parents or felt that they didn't have my best interest at heart.

Have you had those thoughts before?

I wonder about my grandparents and great-grandparents. Each generation plays a massive role in the next generation's success. I wonder how life was when my parents were babies. Have you ever taught about your parent's childhood? Have you ever thought about how their childhood impacts the decisions they make for your family?

Let's actually take a moment and try to picture your parents as babies. Continue to keep an opened mind.

As babies, this was a time in their lives when there was no hesitation about what they wanted. As babies, your parents spit out the foods they didn't like, and happily ate the ones they did. They had no problem expressing their needs and wants. They cried loudly, with no holding back until they got what they wanted. Your parents had everything inside of them that they needed to get fed, changed, held, and rocked. As they got older, they began to crawl around and move toward whatever held their attention the most. They were clear about what they wanted and headed straight towards it with no fear.

So, what happened?

Well, somewhere along the way, someone said,

Don't touch that it will hurt you!

Stay away from the road.

Keep your hands off that.

Eat those vegetables on your plate, whether you like them or not!

You should be ashamed of yourself thinking in that way.

You don't really feel that way.

Do you really think you need that?

Stop being a baby.

As they got older, they began to hear…

Can you think of anybody but yourself?

You can't have everything you want just because you want it

Money doesn't grow on trees!

Stop being so selfish

Start doing what I ask, I am in charge!

Does this baby example sound familiar to you? Have some of these things been said to you? Have you ever taken the time to think about the fact that your parents were once in your shoes?

You may start to realize that your parents thoughts, perceptions, and behaviors were shaped by their culture, their own parents' beliefs, and life circumstances.

I pray that you have a fantastic relationship with your parents. If you don't, I pray that you find it in your heart to realize that your parents are trying to *figure this world out just like you.*

They don't have all the answers

They only have the answers that were taught to them. Some of our parents had terrific upbringings and developed good morals and values, while others were limited to having good morals and values growing up. I encourage you to use the baby example during the times you feel you cannot forgive your parents, for the hurt they caused you. Realize that they could have possibly endured the same circumstances and have not figured out how to overcome them yet.

This book has been written to help you to hold on to your wants and desires, as well as overcome those inner thoughts, beliefs, images, and behaviors that are limiting your success.

I became a parent officially on August 15, 2015, so I feel like I have a little knowledge on how it works.

My baby girl, Zuri is only two as I write this chapter, so I haven't had the pleasure of dealing with boys trying to knock on my door to take her out to the movies, questions about tattoos, or her asking me to teach her how to drive! Still, I have learned early on that when you become a parent, you suddenly seem to gain some knowledge and understanding of why your parents act the way they did growing up. Some of it is surprising.

I personally believe your parents want the best for you. They love you in a way you can't know until you have your own children. In some circumstances, they can make some decisions that you feel are not in your best interest. Yet, deep down, they still love you and want the best for you! I'm telling you, it never made sense until I was in their position.

Suddenly, this little baby is growing inside my wife Amy's belly, doing Kung Fu kicks, and punches, ready to break out. It is a fantastic feeling, having my hand on my wife's belly. As I write this chapter, my wife, Amy is pregnant again, with our second child. It is another girl by the way (yay!)

As I look at my wife going through this experience again, she is such a strong woman. She's been dealing with being sick the entire time through both pregnancies. She experiences throwing up, tiredness, muscles spasms, and weakness daily. It has been so overwhelming, that she has laid in bed for the entire day sometimes. Despite the difficulties, she is so proud to be a mother. She has told me that she would go through it a hundred times, to be able to see our little girls smile! I respect her so much for what she is willing to endure for our family. My daughters are blessed to have her as a mother.

As I think about my daughters, I imagine how they would admire me, and how I'd teach my girls how to brush their teeth (at least twice a day), be brave when the world tries to break their self-esteem, and to develop authentic respect for themselves and others.

I think every parent wants the best for their children. They love their children with the same unexplainable love. Most parents want their children to be healthy and happy, to follow their dreams, and be successful, good contributors to society.

Parents also want love and respect back.

I know that my daughters and I are going to have our days where I won't understand circumstances better than their mom. However, I can honestly say I don't want them to make the same mistakes I made. I would give my life to keep them from going through some of the things I had to endure as a child. I am sure your parents or guardians feel the same way. Regardless of the situation, they have your best interest at heart.

I want to dive deep into some methods and techniques led by God, that I have learned from biblical studies, as well as many other scholars over the years that can help your parents be successful at helping you be the leader you are called to be.

My goal is to get you started thinking and taking action. I know all of this is easier said than done and tough when you don't have a healthy relationship with your parents. It takes a lot of work and consistency. Believe me, I truly understand. I invite you to remember: action creates truth. At the end of the day, your efforts shape the directions for a positive change for those valuable relationships you want to save for long-term.

So, here we go:

Ways to help your parents be successful in helping you be a leader:

Communicate

I know as a kid, it was tough sharing my thoughts and feelings with others. I grew up in an environment where I learned and adapted to not sharing my true feelings with people. By doing so, I was taught your enemy would get the upper hand on you. Sharing your vulnerable side was considered a weakness.

I have learned over the years that those I looked up to had it all wrong. Exposing yourself is not a sign of weakness, it is a real sign of strength. Communication with parents is key to a healthy relationship. It helps them understand you better. I know as a teen, I had the view that my parents should have already known how I feel. They were kids once.

Parents know what to do in all situations. I have found later in life that is not true either.

Your parents have a lot on their plate. They are responsible for your necessities, providing daily meals for you, clothing, and a place to lay your head at night. They also, try to take care of themselves physically and mentally. Lastly, they must try to lead you on the right path to discovering your true self.

Help your parents remember what it is like being a kid. Adults tend to forget. I encourage you to communicate your perceptions, thoughts, and feelings honestly. Communicate your opinions. At the end of the day, you must follow your parent's rules, but ask yourself, am I making it easier for my parents to understand my wants and needs?

Promote your unique voice and self-expectations.

Be Relatable

Encourage your parents to share their childhood experiences with you. When you begin to share more of what is going on in school, or behind closed doors in your life, expect the same feedback from your parents. Expect to hear how school was for them growing up, or other difficulties you are going through in your teen life. Expect to know how life is as an adult. Also, more importantly, share the good that's happening. Ask them if they can relate!

I know this is easier said than done, but I challenge you to try. As you grow to understand where your parents come from and get an understanding of how they were raised, it can provide some clarity for you on why your parents' act the way they do. When you look at all your parent's mistakes and find that you cannot forgive them, you must say to yourself, *"They learned this behavior somewhere when they were younger, this is not their fault (baby example). They are trying to figure life out just like me. Try to strive and find answers together."*

Doing this will make your relationship stronger. It can also help your parents overcome some adversity and make them better leaders for you.

Limit Being Compared to Others

When necessary, make your parents aware that you don't like to be compared to others. For example: *"You should be more like Johnny, he is planning to pursue business school,"* or, *"You should be more like Sheila, she is very respectable, makes good grades and volunteers in the community on the weekends."*

Those things are great, but you must find your own voice.

I have a story to share when I was in middle school, and this carried into my college years. As you know from previous chapters, I struggled for a long time with truly accepting the way I looked. I have a scar on my forehead since I was five/six years old. When I got to the age that I could wear hats in school, I took advantage of it. Around this time, there was a hip-hop artist that was very popular; Curtis Jackson, better known as 50 Cent. I remember people at school saying I resembled him because we are both dark-skinned, have similar facial features (specifically big teeth), the same smile, and muscular build. We also share the same last name.

I have to admit, I started to believe that I was related to him. I remember daydreaming that he would come home to Forest City for Thanksgiving. I would memorize his music, trying to sound like him. It really became official when my Mom started calling me 50 Cent. Then, my siblings and other family members began calling me 50 Cent. I can remember her buying two of 50 Cent pictures and hanging them up in the front room of the house. As I look back on my journey, that was not healthy for me. I took on that identity because I didn't truly love Chaz for who he was. I latched onto the first thing that I viewed as acceptable to society. In the long run, it resulted in me becoming depressed. I honestly just think my Mom followed the hype because she saw that it was cool. She was getting good feedback with me being a look alike, and she saw that I was somewhat happy with it. She viewed 50 Cent as a successful businessman, and that is what she wanted for me; Success.

Parents are always trying to make their kids happy. Regardless of the circumstance, all parents want to see their children be successful in life.

Sadly, it could be at the expense of controlling the whole outcome.

Maybe you can relate to my story in some way. It could also be them trying to persuade you to follow their unachieved dreams, by going to the college of their choice, or taking over the family business. It is essential that you respect your parents 100%. I truly believe being honest and sharing your thoughts is how you show them respect. Strive to make them aware of the times they are comparing you to someone else and not promoting the real you!

The Two Magical Questions

As you discovered so far in this chapter, the parent-child relationship can be a challenge to maintain. You and your parents are always wondering if you are doing things right. You are personally relying heavily on your parents to prepare you for whatever upcoming challenges you may face. I hope by this point in the chapter you have realized that your parents are relying on you as well. Your behavior is key to maintaining a healthy relationship with your parents.

I want to talk about, what I call the "two magical questions."

I believe these two questions will help you personally, as well as your relationships with parents, family members, close friends, school, work acquaintances, etc. The will help you in a productive way.

So, what are these two magical questions that can improve the quality of every relationship you are in?

Here they are:

1. On a scale of 1 to 10, how would you rate the quality of our relationship during the last week (1-2 weeks/month/quarter/semester/season)?

Here are some different ways the same question has worked for me personally:

On a scale of 1 to 10, how would you rate the conversation or experience we just had? Me as a manager? Me as a therapy instructor? Me as a husband? Me as a father? Me as a teacher? This class? This meal? This book?

Any answer less than a 10 gets the follow-up question:

2.   What would it take to make it a 10?

The second question is where the magic honestly happens. You are showing your parents/guardian that you genuinely care and want to know how to be a better son or daughter. You are expressing how building a healthy relationship will be beneficial in the long-term. Being self-aware of what will satisfy your parents gives you the information you need to do what is necessary to create a winning relationship. I challenge you to make it a habit of ending every important conversation, meeting, class, training, or work week with the two questions in mind! I genuinely believe that they will make your relationships stronger than ever and they will challenge you to take action toward becoming a great leader.

Remember: Action creates Truth.

Life of Earthquakes

I was inspired by a story brought to my attention from a devotional my wife and I read together. I wanted to share it with you because I personally feel we all should strive to have a parent-child relationship bond like the one in the story. The story was about a devastating earthquake that occurred on December 7, 1988 in Armenia. It was estimated that 25,000 individuals died that day. In a small town after the quake, a father rushed to his son's school to make sure he was okay.

When he got there, he found that the earthquake had destroyed the building to the point that there was no sign of life! The father did not have a second thought about turning back, he remembered often telling his son *"No matter what, I will always be there when you need me."*

So, the father began removing rubble from where he believed his son's classroom was. No other parents volunteered to help; they would often tell the father to go home. They told him all the children are dead and there is no way the children survived. The father continued to dig, remembering what he promised his son that he would always be there.

After 38 hours of digging, the story says that the father lifted a heavy piece of rubble where he heard in a "tent-like hole", voices, and saw his son! The father saved 14 children, including his son that day.

What hit home for me was the son then said to his father, "*I told the other kids not to worry. I told 'em that if you were alive, you'd save me, and when you saved me, they will be saved. You promised you would always be there for me! You did it, Dad!*"

This story fired me up as a father, and I am sure it fired up the kid that was saved by a father that kept his promise. It made me think about the parent that I am striving to be and how I want my kids to believe in me. I want them always to feel that I will be there for them, as long as I have breath in my body, led by God. I encourage you to remember this story and strive to make your parent-child relationship and love as strong as this father and son, regardless of what earthquakes life throws at you.

In the next chapter, I want to talk about your character and how to take 100% responsibility for your actions moving forward.

Review:

Let's go over some key things you learned about the parent-child relationship in this chapter:

- Helping your parents helps you be successful in your beliefs, visions and goals. It will assist you in living, learning, and leading powerfully.
- Parents are just human beings trying to figure this world out just like you. It is crucial that you understand that!
- Strive to communicate better.
- Strive to be relatable.
- Limit being compared to others.
- Keep in mind the two magical-questions.

Exercise 11: Taking Action

The Perfect Parent Exercise

There can be times, where you are angry and frustrated with your parents, and vice versa.

This exercise that I am about to share is an excellent way to help you have a change of thought and to take your mind back to a more positive state. You care about your parents or guardian, and it is healthy to remind yourself of this fact. I recommend writing this down and posting it in places that you can view easily. Getting a healthy idea about the ones you care about makes a big difference in the way you feel about yourself as well.

Here are the four steps below:

1. List two unique personal qualities (values) you notice about your parent or guardian lives by or follows. Example: *My Dad is Ambitious and Creative.*

2. 2. List one or two ways your parent expresses those qualities above when interacting with you and others. Example: *Support and Inspire.*

3. 3. Imagine that your parent is perfect. The parent has perfect thoughts, relationships, lifestyle, etc. Write a short statement in the present tense of the perfect parent you want to see. How would you like to see them act around your friends, teachers, other families, etc.? Example: *My Dad is very unique and talented. He is hilarious and easy to talk to. Everyone loves him.*

4. 4. Now, combine the three steps above into a single statement. Example: *My Dad uses his ambitious and creative qualities to support and inspire others. My Dad is very unique and talented. He is hilarious and easy to talk to. Everyone loves him.*

Once you have determined and written down your statement, read it every day, preferably in the morning and before bed. Don't be afraid if you are a visual person, put the statement up in your room, bathroom mirror, or on the refrigerator so your parents can see. Imagine how that will raise your parent's self-esteem and confidence. It could improve your relationship with them as well.

The statement you have created has some truth and some things that your parents are not living up to.

I challenge you to remember what I am about to say.

Regardless of your parent's downfalls and struggles, help them by maintaining a perfect picture of them personally. Your thoughts are powerful, and your words towards them are even more powerful. Visualizing the way you want to see your parents on a daily basis can only help them get to that point. Remember to use the two magical questions, we discussed in chapter 11, to help yourself, and help your parents live up to your statement you created.

Chapter 12

Responsible Character

"Your character is the container for your gifts and talents."

Dr. Miles Munroe

As I began writing this chapter, the memory taking our two-year-old daughter Zuri, along with my wife to the circus in Kentucky comes to mind.

They both love elephants, and they had the pleasure of riding on one at the circus. I videotaped the experience. It was funny looking at Zuri's facial expressions. She didn't even cry. I also couldn't help but notice that the trainer had this little rope around this enormous animal; guiding it around in a circle. I thought to myself if this animal truly wanted to act out, it could get loose very quickly, and turn this magical moment into a nightmare!

Something interesting I discovered about a baby elephant is the fact that it is trained at birth to be limited to a tiny space. Its trainer will tie its leg with a rope to a wooden pole planted deep in the ground. This rope limits the baby elephant to an area determined by the length of the rope. The elephant will fight for a period to break away and free itself. However, the rope is too strong, and the baby elephant learns that it can't break it. It becomes accustomed to the fact that it must stay in the area defined by the length of the rope.

As the baby elephant grows into 4-7 ton colossus, it can easily break this rope. However, it doesn't even try, as it has grown up trained to think its strength is limited.

I believe this example of the elephant can relate to human nature. The rope in the example can be limiting beliefs and negative images that you developed when you were younger. At present, they can be shaping your life.

The good news is this can be changed, led by God.

I have discovered on my journey that successful people understand that you are never truly stuck in life. You just keep re-creating the same experiences over and over by thinking the same thoughts, maintaining the same beliefs, speaking the same words, and doing the same things.

It doesn't matter where you are from, or the mistakes you have made. Also, things can be tough to change when you are striving to go beyond your comfort zone. Despite all of that, I truly believe that focusing on who you want to become will shape your character towards living, learning, and leading powerfully, as you are powerfully led by God. I want you to be self-aware of how powerful you are, and how important it is to focus on what you want.

Let's discuss your Character.

Character is defined as the mental and healthy qualities unique to an individual.

You must strive to build your life around values (review chapter 5). Your gifts and talents are as safe as your character. Think of character as being the container for your gifts and talents.

For example, if you had a carton of milk and you added holes in the carton, the fluid will spill out and not be very useful. You wouldn't be able to store the milk without ruining everything else in the fridge. The liquid is only as strong as the carton that's holding it.

Character is the foundation of everything you have learned in this book.

I feel that it is essential for you to address your character at an early age. I challenge you to truly understand what I am about to say:

If you want to be successful, you must take responsibility for everything you experience in life, regardless of the circumstances!

I encourage you to do this right now. This includes all your achievements in and out of school, and the quality of your relationships with classmates, co-workers, family and members. Take responsibility for your health, physical fitness, and your feelings. Start paying attention to your income and potential debt you could be facing early on. Take responsibility for all of it; I mean everything! You are not too young to start this right now!

Let's be 100% real. You have been conditioned to blame something outside of yourself for the parts of your life you don't like. You blame your parents for getting in trouble with the law, or the teachers for not giving you a passing grade in math class. You blame your friends, co-workers, living circumstances, and not having a lot of money for your misfortunes and mistakes. You don't like pointing the finger at yourself. It is easier to blame others.

You are probably like, wow Chaz you are being hard on me. Listen, I have discovered to achieve significant success in life, and develop a responsible character, you must take 100% responsibility for your life. Nothing less will do! I believe you can take 100% responsibility for your life led by God.

Developing good character and taking responsibility means that you are in control of creating the good and the bad in your life. It means you understand that you take responsibility for your experiences. It means you own up to your success and failures. Once you develop the mindset that you have created your current conditions, then you undo them, or you can re-create them, led by God.

I want to spend some time talking about some ways you can continue building responsible character.

Here we go:

Remain A Child at Heart

You know, my daughter Zuri helped me understand a biblical reference that I feel will help provide you a better understanding of remaining a child at heart.

Christ stated, *"Unless you become like little children, you will never enter the Kingdom of Heaven."*

I genuinely believe my two-year-old is consistently expressing the qualities of being in the Kingdom of Heaven daily. She shows love, joy, kindness, goodness, gentleness, and faithfulness within herself. Now, you may say she is young and doesn't know anything, but that's what makes her so unique. That is what makes all children unique. They are innocent and haven't been hit with life experiences yet!

Zuri has a smile that changes any depression in a room instantly. She knows what she wants, and she goes after it. When something happens, for example, she falls at the playground and hurts her knee, she'll cry for a moment and then ask me to discipline the ground (have to pop it, and say *No, don't hurt my Zuri*). Then, she moves on like it never happened.

She doesn't sit there and live in the past or be fearful of trying again. She runs on faith that her father will protect her regardless of the circumstances.

As you get older, I encourage you to keep that little kid inside of you alive. As you go into adult years, you tend to lose sight of your inner child. You get busy with higher-level school, work, family life, and other circumstances. Pay attention and study how children act; I truly believe they are the closest in character to our Creator.

Remain a child at heart.

Learn and Share

As you continue to grow towards becoming your greatest version, share your experiences with others. Your character will grow more and more.

I remember back in 2016, when I acted on my calling and started uploading inspiration and fitness videos. This challenged me to live up to what I was presenting to the public. Stepping outside my comfort zone helped me overcome some addictions that didn't match up to the public figure I envisioned myself becoming!

As you move through high school, and through life, an equal balance of learning and sharing is necessary. You must continue to feed yourself good knowledge and sharing value with others. You are designed to be a natural teacher in an area of gifting! The more you learn in life, you must share at equal value. For example, if I gain the knowledge from a book, it means nothing if I do not create and show action on how that knowledge has impacted me. I must be willing to help someone else. Understanding the value of learning and sharing is the key to building a responsible character and becoming the leader you are destined to be. True wisdom is applied knowledge!

Remember to Floss

I graduated in 2015, with a Degree in Applied Science. I then went on to pass the Physical Therapist Assistant Board Exam. I officially became a Licensed Physical Therapist Assistant. It was one of the most exciting moments of my life. Completing the program helped shape my character the way it is today. One of my goals was to be a traveling therapist assistant. Amy and I wanted to travel and see the more of the United States before little Zuri got older.

The kicker is the fact that I didn't have a Driver's License at the time. Yet, I knew what my heart wanted, and I had my wife's support. I was denied by numerous travel agencies, that thought I was silly for thinking I would get an opportunity to travel without a driver's license. I had one lady that told me, I would never travel with the driving record that I have! I have multiple driving while impaired charges and most agencies felt I was a huge liability. Regardless of what I was told, I knew that the faith I had in Jesus Christ and His unique character and wisdom was stronger than anyone's opinion of me!

I saw a vision of being a traveler in my job field. I expected to make that vision a reality. *With God all things are possible.* I continued to expose my situation to travel agencies, and I finally found one that gave me a chance. I looked adversity in the eyes and wouldn't be denied. One assignment that I took was in a small town, located in Norton, Virginia. I was working at a hospital/outpatient clinic. I learned so much from a great group of individuals.

While I was in the area, Amy and I were due for a general dental follow-up and teeth cleaning. We found a place literally next to where I worked. We had heard good things about the dentist's office. I remember laying in the chair, and the lady, who was about to do the cleaning for me asked me, "How often do you floss your teeth?"

I was honest and told her that I rarely do. She stared at me with a brief pause in speech and stated: *"Did you know when you only brush your teeth, you are only cleaning 45% of your mouth? That means that 55% of your mouth is left unclean unless you floss."*

I told her that I was not aware of this, and it changed my whole perspective on flossing. I can say that I floss daily now. I share this with you because I feel like this percentage can be applied when you think about your public and private life! *I believe 45% of yourself is revealed to the public and 55% of yourself remains private.*

It is human nature to have the tendency to focus on the 45% (which is public life) more than 55% (private life).

Your responsible character is built on your private life.

I challenge you to invest quality time equally between your public and private life. For example, in this story, my public life is built around being a traveling therapist assistant helping others overcome difficulties and improving quality of life. On the other side, my private life is overcoming the challenges of not having a Driver's License. My wife was the only driver, so things were very challenging for both of us mentally and physically. I was continually trying to overcome the limitations of life in private by remaining positive and continuing to learn ways to develop the character my family and clients needed.

Who you are in private is the real you!

Who are you in private? Does it match your public life?

Going back to the dentist story, the lady went on to share that even though your teeth can look clean and you get compliments for your smile, if you are not flossing correctly, plaque and bacteria can grow between your teeth and gums. It can potentially cause gum bleeding as well as premature tooth decay. So, you can literally lose your teeth sooner than you think!

Going back to our public and private lives, if we don't take care of our private lives, it will eventually show up in our public lives.

Let's take a look at Jimmy's life for example:

Jimmy is known as the class act. Jimmy dresses nice and has a great smile when you see him in public. He is very respectable to his teachers and has a lot of friends and people that look up to him in school. Jimmy is the Captain of the football team and was voted Best Athlete by his peers. Everyone wishes they can be a good leader like Jimmy because he has it all together. On the flip side, when Jimmy is not around everyone, his behavior is different. He is sad and depressed most of the time. Jimmy sits in his room and listens to his parents argue every other night. Because he is not happy, he seems to find temporary pleasures in stealing some of his Dad's alcoholic beverages. He also looks at violent images online and watches porn as a comfort to himself. He tends to feel even worse afterward as he thinks about what others would think if they found out. He feels if they knew, him being a leader would fall apart. Jimmy eventually tells himself, no one will find out, and he keeps everything a secret in his private life. Because he feels this way, he rarely invites people to his home, or associates with people outside of school functions.

How do you feel about this example of Jimmy?

Can you relate to him, with your own unique situation?

Even though Jimmy thinks his private life is a secret right now, eventually, everything comes to the public, and his responsible character will be in jeopardy!

I challenge you to be exposed (review chapter six.) Seek people you like and trust, to assist you in striving towards making your private life mirror your public life! Invest quality time in striving to make your private and public life the same. It is the secret to living a long-term healthy, successful life, with responsible character.

Act As If…

We talked about techniques and ways to live, learn, and lead powerfully in this book. Now, I encourage you to act out your desires. It assists in building a responsible character.

Where do you see yourself after middle school or high school? Where do you see yourself after college?

I challenge you to list all of your desires and act as if you have already achieved them. The more you visualize and act out your wishes, the more you create mental feelings and emotions of already having them. In turn, the faster you attract them to you. I encourage students that I talk to and mentor to imagine they are coming back to their 10th Year Class Reunion.

Imagine seeing all your old high school friends standing around and socializing. You are proud to share that you have achieved all your personal desires and goals. You talk about things like your dream career, car, home, or newly discovered gifts and talents. Take it another step and get some of your friends together that you like and trust and role play. You are probably like, *Chaz you are crazy I am not doing that.*

I know this can be challenging if you are more of an introvert like myself. Just remember, on the other side of fear is a safe place.

The more you visualize and act out what you truly want in life, the more you create mental and emotional feelings of already having it, and it will come to reality faster.

Students that have tried this technique have noticed themselves feeling excited, passionate, confident, supportive, generous, happy, self-confident, and content with who they are.

All of these are qualities of a responsible character.

I act out already being one of the top Youth Speakers in the United States. I have saved encouragement comments from people on social media and previous speeches. I view them as messages being sent today.

I send myself numerous emails, addressed by specific schools I want to speak at, telling me they want me to come and inspire their students. I actually have a handmade cover page of this book hanging on my wall and I act as if this book is already finished. I visualize everyone congratulating me, and I am signing endless copies of my book for all of them.

Now, it is possible that you haven't figured all this stuff out and you are probably like *Chaz, I don't know where I want to work or live in ten years. I am just trying to get out of grade school.*

That is okay. As always, I am trying to get you thinking and encourage you to use this technique and adjust it as you begin to discover more about yourself and the things you like. I challenge you to use it in THE NOW!

For example:

- Act as if you already got that A in science class.
- Act as if you have a healthy relationship with your parents.
- Act as if you have overcome the addiction that is holding you back from reaching your goals.
- Act as if your team has already won the championship game.

Let's be clear on one thing, role-playing and visualizing is not enough by itself to change your entire future. **Action creates truth.** You will still have to take the right steps toward your dreams and goals, to make them happen. However, there is one more piece of developing responsible character and away in supporting you in the creation of your desired future:

Be Okay with Uncertainty

I want to share another biblical reference, that I feel will give you a better understanding.

I want to share and paraphrase another biblical reference found in the book of Isaiah. The author of the book talks about how God's thoughts and ways are more significant than our thoughts and ways. In other words, what you hold as truth or beliefs in your minds, the creator of the world is above what you think, or believe. **This is powerful.** I have learned on my journey that as human beings, we should keep living, learning and, leading, but realize that you will never have all the answers! Only the Creator has all the answers.

I repeat, you will never wholly figure this world out. Our Creator's mind is too complicated! You must be okay with the fact that you are not always going to know the answers. Life will bring some mystery

Faith places a huge role in my life. I strive to walk by faith, and not by sight every day.

Keep this in mind!

Again, life will bring mystery for sure. I know at this age, you are trying to figure things out and understand what's going on with your bodies and who you really are. The material that we have covered in this book was written and compiled to last for a lifetime. I pray that you find value in it as you progress into your adult years.

Remember this: life is a marathon, not a sprint! Take it one day at a time as you continue to discover ways to re-create new and improved experiences, thoughts, and beliefs for yourself. They will allow you to be fulfilled in heart and happy in life.

If you genuinely develop the understanding that action creates truth, and keep God first, you will always be on track, in striving to live, learn, and lead powerfully, as you are powerfully led by God.

Review:

- Character can be defined as the mental and healthy qualities you follow that makes you a unique individual.
- Maintaining responsible character is built around values (review chapter 5). I challenge you to:
- Take 100% responsibility for your actions and make known with boldness who you are and how valuable you are to the world
- Remain a child at heart.
- Invest and work towards making your public and private life identical and real.
- Take pride in learning and sharing your desires and goals.
- Act as if you have already achieved your goals.
- Realize that some things in life are going to be uncertain.

Exercise 12: Taking Action

Let's be honest, at some point in your life, you will deal with limiting experiences, thoughts, and beliefs as you progress into your adult years.

These habits can potentially negatively affect your public life.

Below is a problem-solving technique that has worked for me personally. It consists of four questions and a solution that can assist you in overcoming limitations and allow you to develop a strong character to support your gifts and talents in your private and public life.

Get a sheet of paper and write these questions down. As you continue to consistently apply the steps, and honestly believe it is possible to change, you will see a difference.

Be honest with yourself, and don't be afraid to get people you like, and trust involved.

Let's get started.

Conquer Limiting Beliefs

1. Make a list of some beliefs that could be limiting you.
   Example: *Not smart enough to maintain a 3.5 GPA in school.*
2. Determine how the belief limits you.
   Example: *Don't give much effort, because I believe I won't pass anyway.*
3. Decide how you want to be, act, feel.
   Example: *I want to feel confident with my school studies, and willing to reach out for help when needed from teachers and mentors.*
4. Create a different thought or statement that affirms or gives you permission to be, act or feel this way (repeat morning when you wake up and before you go to sleep.)
   Example: *I am confident with my school studies, and I have all the help and resources around me to make a 3.5 GPA. I believe that I can accomplish this goal. I am determined to be successful and willing to help others along the way.*

Final Thoughts

I hope you enjoyed reading *Live, Learn and Lead powerfully, A Teen Leadership Guide*. This book is designed to align your mind towards living, learning, and leading powerfully, as you are powerfully led by God. I am so excited that you invested the time to complete this book.

I want to share a quote from teen motivational speaker Josh Shipp's book, "The Teen's Guide to World Domination" (2010):

> *"The best stories don't end with you. The best stories live on through your friends and family, and the lives you've had an impact on. That's the thing about living a great life. It's infectious."*

I pray that you develop an *infectious character* that empower others in your environment and you consistently apply the principles and values learned in this book, in your life right now.

With confidence, I can say as I sit and type this passage, and hold baby Mila in my lap, this book has changed my life physically and mentally. I know if you truly read and took this book seriously it has changed yours as well!

As an adult, **I will read this book throughout the rest of my lifetime**, and **I challenge you** to do the same as you progress in years.

I am so grateful and blessed to have the opportunity to inform, inspire and empower you with the tools and problem-solving techniques needed to overcome adversity and accomplish your dreams and goals.

In this final thought, I want to encourage you to picture the life you want to live, and regardless of what life throws your way, continue to know with God leading your life, all things are possible to overcome and become if…

"*You Believe.*"

Find the best ways to take the first step, and then the second, third, fourth, and so on. Learn to stay on course along the way. Before long, perhaps a lot sooner than you expect, you will live, learn and lead powerfully in whatever area your heart desires. God Bless!

Teen/Young Adult Resources

AMERICORPS

Assists in providing hundreds of National and Local programs that address community needs in education, disaster services, human services, public and environmental safety.

www.americorps.org

BOYS & GIRLS CLUBS OF AMERICA

Provide opportunities in developing leadership skills, knowledge, and career studies to the youth. They take pride in enhancing health and life skills, financial literacy, as well as providing arts, sports, fitness, recreation, and family outreach services.

www.bgca.org

BOY SCOUTS OF AMERICA

This is one of the most extensive scouting organizations in America. It includes character-development and leadership training programs for youth, serving millions of young people between the ages of 7 and 21 years of age.

www.scouting.org

DO SOMETHING

This is a well-known National Non-Profit organization that assists over 6 million youth and young adults in developing leadership skills and ways to build and transform their community.

www.dosomething.org

EARTH FORCE

They inspire young people to become problem-solvers in their communities by noticing environmental issues and increasing awareness involving science.

www.earthforce.org

EPA STUDENT CENTER

They offer grade school students (K-12) the chance to explore and build interest in a wide range of environmental issues, as well as resources on awards, scholarships, internships, club projects, and other fun activities.

www.epa.gov/students

GIRL SCOUTS OF AMERICA

They help young women as the world's renowned organization dedicated to character-building and developing leaders for the next generation. The primary focus is to assist girls in thriving towards developing a strong sense of self, positive values, overcoming adversity, and becoming contributors to their communities.

www.girlscouts.org

HABITAT FOR HUMANITY

This is a passionate organization that assists in bringing volunteers and communities together to build affordable housing for people in need. It offers different programs for students across America.

www.habitat.org

JUNIOR ACHIEVEMENT

This is a dedicated organization that takes pride in developing young people and preparing them for success in a global economy.

www.ja.org

MENTAL HEALTH ISSUES FOR KIDS AND TEENS

This is an authoritative resource that offers articles and book reviews for children and adolescents interested in exploring and understanding mental health issues. They provide information on Depression, Attention Deficit Disorder (ADHD), and Separation Anxiety Disorder.

www.ncpamd.com

NATIONAL INSTITUTE OF DRUG ABUSE

They aid in helping young people learn about the effects of drug abuse on the body and brain.

www.teens.drugabuse.gov

SUMMER JOBS

This is a useful tool to use to find work in your area. Browse through the job postings, submit a resume, or just add yourself to the email list to get updates.

www.summerjobs.com

THE COLLEGE BOARD

This resource offers information on colleges, scholarships opportunities and how to find them, as well as the SATs and PSATs resources and career services.

www.collegeboard.org

THE NATIONAL FOUNDATION FOR TEACHING ENTREPRENEURSHIP (NFTE)

They help young people from low-income communities explore and learn about business and ways to enhance entrepreneurial skills.

www.nfte.com

THE NATIONAL MENTORING PARTNERSHIP

The well-known organization that aid in helping young people find a mentor and grow mentoring opportunities around the country.

www.mentoring.org

TEEN ANON

A great resource in helping teens with drinking and drug issues, as well as all those who love them.

www.teen-anon.com

THE WRITE SOURCE

This resource offers ideas and opportunities for writing projects, examples of teen writing, and a chance to have your work published.

www.thewritesource.com

YOUTH ACTIVISM PROJECT

A well-known organization that operates 100% volunteer, who inspires the youth to participate in community problems related to misconduct, health, education, environmental issues, etc.

www.youthactivism.com

Notes

Introduction:

Alsbrooks, B. (2017). Blessed and unstoppable: Your blueprint for success. Deland, FL: Positive Worldwide Publishing.

Canfield, J., & Switzer, J. (2015). *The success principles: How to get from where you are to where you want to be.* New York: William Morrow.

Matthew 5:47-48 ICB. (n.d.). Retrieved from https://www.bible.com/bible/1359/mat.5.47-48.icb

Munroe, M. (1999) *In Pursuit of Purpose – The Key To Personal Fulfilment, Destiny Image Pub.*

Chapter 1:

BibleGateway. (n.d.). Retrieved from https://www.biblegateway.com/passage/?search=Genesis 2:8-25&version=NIV

BibleGateway. (n.d.). Retrieved from https://www.biblegateway.com/passage/?search=2 Corinthians 4:7&version=NASB

Matthew 5:47-48 ICB. (n.d.). Retrieved from https://www.bible.com/bible/1359/mat.5.47-48.icb

Munroe, M. (1999) *In Pursuit of Purpose – The Key To Personal Fulfilment,* Destiny Image Pub

Success for Teens: Real teens talk about using the slight edge. (2008). Lake Dallas, TX: Success Books/Video Plus L.P.

Chapter 2:

BibleGateway. (n.d.). Retrieved from https://www.biblegateway.com/passage/?search=gal 5:22-23&version=NASB

Canfield, J., & Switzer, J. (2015). *The success principles: How to get from where you are to where you want to be.* New York: William Morrow.

Shipp, J. (2010). *The teen's guide to world domination: Advice on life, liberty, and the pursuit of awesomeness.* New York: St. Martins Griffin.

Chapter 3:

Alsbrooks, B. (2017). Blessed and unstoppable: Your blueprint for success. Deland, FL: Positive Worldwide Publishing.

BibleGateway. (n.d.). Retrieved from https://www.biblegateway.com/passage/?search=Romans 12:2&version=NASB

Covey, S. (2016). *The 7 habits of highly effective teens the ultimate teenage success guide.* Halifax, Nova Scotia: Atlantic Provinces Special Education Authority, Library.

Chapter 4:

Alsbrooks, B. (2017). Blessed and unstoppable: Your blueprint for success. Deland, FL: Positive Worldwide Publishing.

BibleGateway. (n.d.). Retrieved from https://www.biblegateway.com/passage/?search=Proverbs 29:18&version=NASB Galatians 6:9-10 NASB

BibleGateway. (n.d.). Retrieved from https://www.biblegateway.com/passage/?search=2 Corinthians 5:7&version=NASB

How Success is Like a Chinese Bamboo Tree. (2017, January 04). Retrieved from https://www.mattmorris.com/how-success-is-like-a-chinese-bamboo-tree/

Ra, Naazir. (2011). *The Hidden Self: A guide to the metaphysical self* 2nd Edition Georgia: Luminous Publications

Chapter 5:

BibleGateway. (n.d.). Retrieved from https://www.biblegateway.com/passage/?search=Joshua 1:8-9&version=NASB

Usmar, J., & Hibbert, Jessamy Dr (2015). *This book will make you confident.* London: Quercus Editions.

Vanderzyden, Chris (2012). *A-z Blueprint for Success A Strategy of Action Steps to Elevate Your Business and Life.* Balboa Pr.

Chapter 6:

Bible Gateway passage: Hebrews 10:24-25 - New American Standard Bible. (n.d.). Retrieved from https://www.biblegateway.com/passage/?search=Hebrews 10:24-25;&version=NASB

Canfield, J., & Switzer, J. (2015). *The success principles: How to get from where you are to where you want to be.* New York: William Morrow.

2 Corinthians 8. (n.d.). Retrieved from https://bible.org/seriespage/2-corinthians-8

Chapter 7:

Bible Gateway passage: Hebrews 10:24-25 - New American Standard Bible. (n.d.). Retrieved from https://www.biblegateway.com/passage/?search=Hebrews 10:24-25;&version=NASB

Vanderzyden, Chris (2012). *A-z Blueprint for Success A Strategy of Action Steps to Elevate Your Business and Life.* Balboa Pr.

Usmar, J., & Hibbert, Jessamy Dr (2015). *This book will make you confident.* London: Quercus Editions.

Chapter 8:

BibleGateway. (n.d.). Retrieved from https://www.biblegateway.com/passage/?search=Genesis 2:7&version=NASB

BibleGateway. (n.d.). Retrieved from https://www.biblegateway.com/passage/?search=gal 5:22-23&version=NASB

BibleGateway. (n.d.). Retrieved from https://www.biblegateway.com/passage/?search=2 Corinthians 4:7&version=NASB

Success for Teens: Real teens talk about using the slight edge. (2008). Lake Dallas, TX: Success Books/Video Plus L.P.

Chapter 9:

BibleGateway. (n.d.). Retrieved from https://www.biblegateway.com/passage/?search=Galatians 5:16-26&version=NASB

Total Transformation Program | Parent Help for Defiant Children. (n.d.). Retrieved from https://www.empoweringparents.com/product/total-transformation-program/

Chapter 10:

BibleGateway. (n.d.). Retrieved from https://www.biblegateway.com/passage/?search=Proverbs 19-21&version=NASB

Canfield, J., & Switzer, J. (2015). *The success principles: How to get from where you are to where you want to be.* New York: William Morrow.

Sanborn, M. (2008). *The Fred Factor.* London: Cornerstone Digital.

Shipp, J. (2010). *The teen's guide to world domination: Advice on life, liberty, and the pursuit of awesomeness.* New York: St. Martins Griffin.

Vanderzyden, Chris (2012). *A-z Blueprint for Success A Strategy of Action Steps to Elevate Your Business and Life*. Balboa Press.

35 Printable Resume Templates. (n.d.). Retrieved from https://www.template.net/business/letters/printable-resume-template/

43 New Stock Of High School Resume Sample. (n.d.). Retrieved from https://frokennilssonskok.com/high-school-resume-sample/

Chapter 11:

Akbar, N. (1996). *Breaking the chains of psychological slavery*. Tallahassee, FL: Mind Productions & Associates.

Dungy, T., & Whitaker, N. (2011). *The one-year uncommon life daily challenge*. Carol Stream, IL: Tyndale House.

Evans, T. (2014). *Raising kingdom kids*. Carol Stream, IL: Tyndale House.

Chapter 12:

Bible Gateway passage: Isaiah 55:8-9 - New American Standard Bible. (n.d.). Retrieved from https://www.biblegateway.com/passage/?search=Isaiah 55:8-9&version=NASB

Canfield, J., & Switzer, J. (2015). *The success principles: How to get from where you are to where you want to be*. New York: William Morrow.

Kleon, A. (2012). *Steal like an artist: 10 things nobody told you about being creative*. New York: Workman Publishing Company.

Matthew 5:48 (RSV). (n.d.). Retrieved from https://www.blueletterbible.org/rsv/mat/5/48/s_934048

Matthew 19:26 NIV. (n.d.). Retrieved from https://www.biblica.com/bible/?osis=niv:matt.19.26

Shipp, J. (2010). *The teens guide to world domination: Advice on life, liberty, and the pursuit of awesomeness*. New York: St. Martins Griffin.

Made in United States
North Haven, CT
05 July 2022